THE ROYAL GLOUCESTERSHIRE HUSSARS

Sir Algar Howard MC of Thornbury Castle was commissioned into the Carmarthen
(Royal Garrison Artillery) Militia in 1900 and rose to the rank of captain before
transferring to RGH in 1908, accepting the rank of 2nd Lt. in true Yeomanry spirit. He
was troop leader of the Oldown Troop, D Sqn on the outbreak of the First World War
and was one of the few officers who had mobilized with the Regiment in 1914 to serve
right through to the entry into Aleppo in 1918. He was awarded the MC for gallantry in
Palestine in 1917. His diary of life with the RGH provided Frank Fox with much of the
detail for his *History of the RGHY 1898–1922* and for captions in his book.

THE ROYAL
GLOUCESTERSHIRE
HUSSARS

ROLLO CLIFFORD

ALAN SUTTON

First published in the United Kingdom in 1991 by
Alan Sutton Publishing Ltd · Phoenix Mill · Far Thrupp · Stroud · Gloucestershire

First published in the United States of America in 1992 by
Alan Sutton Publishing Inc. · Wolfeboro Falls · NH 03896–0484

British Library Cataloguing in Publication Data

Clifford, Rollo
The Royal Gloucestershire Hussars
I. Title
357.10941

ISBN 0 86299 982 0

Library of Congress Cataloging in Publication Data applied for

Cover illustration: The RGH Yeomanry Cavalry at Patcham Camp, 1914.

Half-title page:
*Henry Somerset, Marquis of Worcester, later 7th Duke of Beaufort, the first Commanding
Officer of the Gloucestershire Yeomanry Cavalry. He had seen regular service with the 10th
Royal Hussars in the Peninsula War under Wellington. He was offered command of the
newly-formed regiment in 1834 at the historic meeting at Petty France at which the
independent troops within the county were formed into one regiment. He served as CO
until his death in 1853.*

Title-page:
*This was the first guidon to be presented to the RGH. It was presented on 27 May 1962 by
the Honorary Colonel, the 10th Duke of Beaufort on behalf of HM The Queen. Guidons
were swallow-tailed flags carried by French light cavalry and are equivalent to the standards
of heavy cavalry regiments and colours of infantry battalions. British Light Dragoons took
to them in Napoleonic times. Whereas the colour is always carried by a subaltern, the
guidon is borne by a SNCO. The guidon was the regimental rallying flag and bears the
Regiment's Battle Honours, most of which are described in the following pages. In regular
regiments, guidons are replaced approximately every twenty-five years.*

Typeset in Times 10/12.
Typesetting and origination by
Alan Sutton Publishing Limited.
Printed in Great Britain by
The Bath Press, Avon.

Foreword by

Colonel The Duke of Beaufort MFH

My family became connected with the Gloucestershire Yeomanry Cavalry, as it was known at that time, in 1834 when the then Marquis of Worcester, later the 7th Duke, was offered command of the newly combined independent troops of the yeomen of the County.

Since then members of my family have served continuously to the present day either as members, commanding officers or Honorary Colonels.

The longest serving of these was 'Master' the 10th Duke, who was Honorary Colonel for 59 years from 1925 until his death in 1984.

I take great pride in the fact that the regiment, now represented by Squadrons within the Royal Wessex Yeomanry, continues to wear my family livery of blue and buff and the Portcullis as their cap badge.

Beaufort

October 1991.

INTRODUCTION

Gloucestershire is a maritime county, as visitors to the Regimental Museum in the Customs House at the docks in Gloucester are made aware. The county was among the first to form troops of volunteer yeomanry cavalry on William Pitt's appeal when Napoleon threatened invasion. In 1795 Mr Powell Snell of Guiting Grange raised the First or Cheltenham Troop of Gloucestershire Gentlemen and Yeomanry, making us just a year younger than our friends in Wiltshire, the senior yeomanry regiment, although there was a short break in the continuity of the Gloucestershire troops between 1828 and 1830. Other troops rapidly followed Cheltenham, at Minchinhampton, Wotton-under-Edge and Stow-on-the-Wold, whose standard of 1797 survives, of crimson silk, edged with gold and inscribed *Cotswold Volunteers*.

There was no need to conscript cavalry in accordance with the government's Provisional Cavalry Act as further troops were formed at Henbury, two in Bristol, Stroud, and, in 1797, Captain Robert Morris founded his Gloucester Troop, which he commanded up to his death in 1816. His portrait can be seen in the museum in Gloucester, wearing a black leather helmet and red jacket, which stands nearby with the Troop Standard, embroidered RGYC, for Royal Gloucester Yeomanry Cavalry. Their medical officer was the eminent surgeon Charles Brandon Trye, whose conspicuous monument is in the cathedral. They met at the Bell Inn in Gloucester in 1797 and their drill book containing their rules still survives. Volunteers were exempt from tax on horses and hair powder.

In 1803 as Napoleon concentrated the Grande Armée at Boulogne to invade, the yeomanry undertook beacon duty and several old troops were revived. Earl Bathurst commanded the new Cirencester Troop of 1803 and Dursley, Grumbold's Ash (near Badminton), Tewkesbury, Tortworth and Winterbourne Troops were formed. The Lords Lieutenant were responsible for the readiness of the yeomanry, the Earl of Berkeley in Gloucestershire and the Duke of Beaufort in Monmouthshire, where the Chepstow and Monmouth Troops of the Gloucester Yeomanry Cavalry were first raised in 1798. The latter was led by Captain Richard Lewis, squire of Llantillio, renowned for commanding 'with the language of the hunting field, . . . hardly consistent with the usual system of military etiquette' and for his Troop's 'midnight frolics'. One of the early photographs is of the Monmouth Troop in 1875.

What manner of men were these loyal volunteers, who, as early as 1798, agreed to the Lord Lieutenant's request to serve in case of invasion beyond the county with their own horses, the government usually, but not always, providing arms and accoutrements? The yeoman is traditionally a countryman and a farmer, good with a horse and a gun, who makes a natural member of a light cavalry troop, a skilful rider and marksman. The English never tolerate large standing armies (as we can see at this present time) and our freedom depends not only on our island geography, but on our swift ability to form locally organized militia, usually volunteer or conscript infantry in the towns and volunteer cavalry from the countryside.

This historic sequence of photographs, carefully selected from the surprisingly rich family records of generations of yeomen in peace and war, as well as regimental archives, captures moments in the military life of essentially non-professional soldiers. These are amateurs in the best sense, who volunteered, and still volunteer today, to train in peacetime to defend their county and their country in times of trouble and danger. This yeomanry spirit is characterized by enthusiasm and the enjoyment of the hard work required to achieve professional cavalry standards in war. Readers of Major W.H. Wyndham-Quin's *The Yeomanry Cavalry of Gloucestershire and Monmouth* (1898), of which he was adjutant from 1889 to 1895, which traces the detailed history of the first hundred years, cannot fail to note the emphasis placed on excellence in training and manoeuvres, then as now, highly prized by the yeomen and consistently noted by inspecting officers throughout the nineteenth century. This enthusiasm for high standards, combined with the comradeship born of sharing drills and camps, enabled the Royal Gloucestershire Hussars to acquit themselves with distinction in the Boer War and in two World Wars.

The yeomanry role was at first also that of mounted police, to contain civil unrest which threatened, for example, soon after the French Revolution and again in the 1830s following the resentment against agricultural machinery and the riots preceding the 1832 Reform Bill. The Gloucester Troop dealt with an affray of Irish Militia and citizens at the Swan Inn in 1810 and the Monmouth and Chepstow Troops were three times commended for speedily turning out to deal with colliers' riots in South Wales in 1822, using the flat of their swords to good effect. Seven troops were revived in 1831, notably Captain William Codrington's Marshfield and Dodington Troop, who rode, forty strong, sixteen miles to arrive at the height of the Bristol Riots, only to be sent home undeployed by the incompetent regular officer in charge. The Tetbury Troop spent a week in the city in aid of the civil power.

In 1834 the Troop commanders met at Petty France and decided to combine into a regiment, choosing as their first commanding officer the Marquis of Worcester, soon to become 7th Duke of Beaufort, a 10th Hussar who had served under Wellington in the Peninsula. Thus began the regiment's close connection with Badminton and, nearly a hundred and fifty years later, the 11th Duke of Beaufort, our Honorary Colonel, continues the tradition of five generations of the Somerset family. Yeomanry service is a family affair. These photographs portray person-alities from all walks of life in Gloucestershire, especially the farming and land-owning community; the Cliffords of Frampton (four generations), the Bathursts at Cirencester, the Yorkes from Forthampton; Bristol families like the Harfords and the Harveys; the families Ponsonby, Ashton, Hicks Beach and Elwes; the Barton family pictured here from the Berkeley Vale and the Marsdens, Beards and Pearces, who have served recently.

The early troops wore Light Dragoon uniforms, varying from blue to scarlet coats, white breeches and black leather helmets and carried pistols and swords, first straight then curved sabres. Twelve muzzle-loading carbines per troop were carried by the 'skirmishers' until the first Westley Richards breech-loading carbines were introduced in 1861 (fully adopted in 1871, replaced by Sniders in 1879 and by Martini Henrys in 1886). By 1834 the uniform was a scarlet double-breasted tunic and blue sash, blue trousers with red stripes and a chaco with black plume (at first Prussian then Austrian style), as worn in the equestrian portraits of the 7th Duke of Beaufort as Colonel and of Sir William Codrington at Dodington in the 1840s.

In 1841 the royal title was granted by Queen Victoria. The change to the characteristic blue Hussar uniform, still worn today as full dress, came in 1847 and the Regiment became known as the Royal Gloucestershire Hussars. For some years the Duke of Beaufort insisted that the slung jacket be worn over the back, Hungarian fashion, instead of over the shoulder. In 1860 the busby replaced the chaco and in 1867 pantaloons and boots replaced the old riding overalls. After 1882 the slung jacket was no longer worn by NCOs and privates. Some of these changes can be detected in the photographs of the last century, the earliest of which date from the 1860s. The result of the Duke of Beaufort's order in 1846 that yeomen should grow moustachios, caused some merriment in the pages of *Punch* at the time and is readily discernable in these photographs.

After the bad agricultural years of the 1870s and '80s, volunteer numbers increased again and yeomanry life in the 1890s and early years of this century was extremely active, judging by the wealth of material from which the editors had to choose. The Prince of Wales' visit to Cheltenham in 1897 crowns the period leading up to the first time the RGH saw active service, in the Boer War, which unfortunately is not well recorded.

Early in 1900 a squadron made up of 125 yeomen trained at Horfield Barracks, Bristol and were equipped by the Lord Lieutenant's committee as mounted infantry, in khaki with slouch hats and heavy web bandoliers and armed with Lee-Metford rifles. They formed the 3rd Company of the 1st Battalion Imperial Yeomanry and took twenty days to reach Capetown from Liverpool with their horses. Camp conditions were bad and the yeomen suffered from dysentery and fever. A brief account of their part in the campaign is in Frank Fox's *History of the RGH Yeomanry, 1898–1922* and a map is included later in this book that shows their progress. Long treks, sickness and short rations accounted for more casualties than the enemy, and the yeomen were under fire sixty-five times before returning home in July 1901.

In April 1901 Lee Enfield rifles and bayonets replaced swords and carbines, but the Duke of Beaufort obtained permission for swords to be retained for ceremonial occasions. Cavalry warfare and tactics were changing with the advent of longer range firearms and with Boer War experience. In 1903 the blue Hussar uniform gave way to service dress with blue collars, shoulder straps, puttees and slouch hats, a most unpopular move. Full dress was happily restored again in 1906 for ceremonial occasions up to the First World War, but with Beaufort blue peaked caps instead of busbys for the yeomen. Annual camps at Badminton, Winchcombe, Cirencester, and others, are well documented here. 'The officers . . . are good riders' and 'the NCOs and men ride boldly and well' wrote an inspecting officer. But the real test of horsemastership was to come in the heat, thirst, fatigue and flies of the Sinai Desert and the last great cavalry campaign in history under General Allenby. However, the RGH were at first obliged to abandon their horses in Egypt and fight dismounted as infantry in the catastrophic final effort of the Gallipoli campaign. No-one who has listened to surviving yeomens' accounts can be left in any doubt, as to its misconception and waste and we paid heavily for our participation. Small comfort that the yeomanry, coming up as reserves under no cover at all, earned undying praise from the professional commanders for amazing steadiness of movement under heavy fire.

Qatia was altogether a different kind of disaster, where, on 23 April 1916, A Squadron (five officers and one hundred and one men) were overcome by a vastly overwhelming Turkish force and could not be relieved. Four officers and sixteen yeomen were killed, with twenty-five wounded and two officers and sixty-one yeomen taken prisoner. Five Military Medals were awarded for gallantry. Only nine RGH managed to get away, including the severely wounded Sergeant Charles Lovell who was rescued immobile like a sprout bag, and survived, later to run the Old Comrades Association from 1922 to the 1970s.

This successful, but arduous, cavalry campaign is well recorded in photographs, covering all aspects of life in Palestine. For this period the author has drawn heavily on such important sources as the excellent album of Corporal Hugh Walwin and from the graphic accounts given by Frank Fox and by Sir Algar Howard in his diary. Sir Algar, from the moment he mobilised his troop 'of 20–25 farmers living within a radius of six miles of Thornbury' in three hours, to hunting jackals with his favourite hound, Tripe, in Syria after the armistice, describes in fascinating detail five years of the RGH at war in the Middle East. Fortunately, he too carried a camera. He describes the enormous efforts to find water for the horses, who sometimes went without for three days, when all movement depended on them. Disease and fatigue limited the pace of cavalry pursuit and dysentery was held at bay with Horlick's malted milk, provided by Major G.N. Horlick, who was among those who gave their lives, dying of malaria at Alexandria in 1918. The final sacrifice was 228 men. The RGH eventually returned to Gloucester in August 1919.

In the same year that the war memorial was unveiled on College Green in 1922, mechanisation arrived. The 21st (RGH) Armoured Car Company (TA) Royal Tank Corps was equipped wth the Peerless armoured car armed with two Vickers guns, replaced in 1928–9 by the faster and much-loved Rolls Royces. In 1938, the regiment regained its former title of Royal Gloucestershire Hussars. Numbers had been mounting again with the threat of war with Germany and two regiments were created in the following year, when over one thousand yeomen attended camp at Tidworth.

Home defence and training was to be the invaluable role of 1st RGH, most of whose members served in action and, although eventually equipped with Churchill tanks and prepared for the Far East, armistice came before deployment and the regiment was sent to Austria. Here their full dress musical ride in Vienna in 1945 lived up to the RGH style typified in these pages. 2nd RGH, in spite of having trained for many years with armoured cars, became an armoured regiment in 1939 and, as part of 22nd Armoured Brigade, an entirely yeomanry brigade, were equipped with Crusader tanks, with two pounders and Besas, reaching Suez in October 1941. Lieutenant-Colonel Stuart Pitman's elegantly written *Second Royal Gloucestershire Hussars, Libya – Egypt 1941–1942*, is a classic account, modest but vivid, of what was nothing less than a heroic campaign. Here is the Western desert, with its heat, sandstorms, scorpions and mosquitos, thirst and short rations, and very cold nights. The RGH were frequently outnumbered, out-armoured and out-gunned but they fought hard and professionally and were extremely effective.

During its year of fighting the Regiment, sharing in the triumphs and disasters of the Eighth Army, took its part in the great five hundred mile advance to the western confines of Cyrenaica, the valiant failure at Knightsbridge, the retreat to el Alamein, and the final stopping of the Afrika Corps at the battle of Alam el Halfa. 'The casualty lists – ever a sign of a Regiment's courage – and indeed the awards, vouch for the Gloucestershire Yeomanry's record', wrote the 10th Duke of Beaufort, in his foreword to Tim Pitman's book. Without the campaign of 1941–2, as someone succinctly put it, 'there wouldn't have been no last battle of Alamein nor no Africa Star'.

The RGH, eager and well-trained, got into a great battle on their first morning in action at Bir el Gubi and suffered serious casualties, losing thirty tanks against heavy odds and longer fire power. Lieutenant Tom Elder-Jones' description of his part of the fighting is more poignant than any surviving photograph. Cameras were, of course, forbidden on active service, more strictly it seems than in the previous war, but no-one has time to use a camera in the middle of a tank battle. Most of these desert records show brief moments of pause or resting. Crusaders were replaced by Honeys and Grants with their 75 mm guns. After Alam el Halfa and much sacrifice, the RGH were not permitted to fight again as a Regiment, but its members fought on with others through to the end of the war with Germany, Lieutenant-Colonel Sam Lloyd commanding the Wiltshire Yeomanry. Many yeomen took commissions in other regiments. A faithful representation of Colonel Tony Holloway's Crusader features as a display in the museum in Gloucester.

For those of us too young to have seen a shot fired in anger, post-war National Service and Territorial Army soldiering, with the Daimlers, the Dingos and the Ferrets, the ever-changing roles allotted to the RGH are recalled here in such highlights as the Badminton Horse Trials, the Guidon parade at Badminton in 1962 and the Freedom of Gloucester ceremony. The Regiment's close concern with horses and hunting continues today, fostered by Master, the 10th Duke of Beaufort, who, as Honorary Colonel for fifty-nine years, kept the interests of the Royal Gloucestershire Hussars and Yeomanry close to his heart, proud that his regiment would always maintain the long yeomanry tradition of willingness and readiness 'should there ever be the dreadful necessity of drawing the sword'.

Anthony Mitchell TD

Lieutenant H.J. Clifford at Frampton *c.* 1865. He had served as a midshipman in HMS *Blenheim* during the Baltic Campaign of 1855 and was later commissioned into the RGH in 1865. He was the great-grandfather of the author.

The Right Honourable Henry John Earl of Ducie
Lord Lieutenant of the County of Gloucester and of the City and County of
the City of Gloucester and of the City and County of the City of Bristol
To Cornet Henry James Clifford.

By Virtue of the Statute passed in the forty fourth year of the reign of His late Majesty King George the Third "To consolidate and amend the provisions of the several Acts relating to Corps of Yeomanry in Great Britain and to make further regulations relating thereto" and in exercise of the power and authority to me given I the said Henry John Earl of Ducie by and with the approbation of Her Majesty do by this writing under my hand constitute, appoint and commission you the said Henry James Clifford to be Lieutenant in the Royal Gloucestershire Regiment of Hussar Yeomanry but not to take rank in the Army except during the time of the said Regiment being carried out into actual Service You are therefore carefully and diligently to discharge the duty of Lieutenant by exercising and well disciplining both the inferior Officers and Soldiers of that Regiment who are hereby commanded in Her Majesty's Name to obey you as their Lieutenant And you are to observe and follow such Orders and Directions as you shall from time to time receive from Her Majesty or any other your superior Officer pursuant to the Regulations of the Statutes in that case made and according to the Rules and Discipline of War in pursuance of the trust hereby reposed in you

Given under my hand this twenty fourth day of August in the twenty ninth year of the reign of our Sovereign Lady Queen Victoria And in the year of our Lord One thousand eight hundred and sixty five

Ducie

H.J. Clifford's commission into the Royal Gloucestershire Regiment of Hussar Yeomanry, signed by Lord Ducie of Tortworth, the then Lord Lieutenant, on 24 August 1865.

The Dodington Troop, Royal Gloucestershire Hussars Yeomanry Cavalry, 1869. To the fore are Lieutenant Sir Gerald Codrington, Sergeant-Major Cooper and Captain the Lord

Raglan, whose father was Commander-in-Chief in the Crimea and before that, as Lord Fitzroy Somerset, was Chief of Staff to Wellington during the Peninsula War.

A group of yeomen of the Monmouth Troop, C Sqn RGHY in 1875.

The Lloyd-Lindsay Cup, 1888. The picture shows the team from the E (Gloucester) Troop RGH who won the Lloyd-Lindsay Challenge Cup for the fourth consecutive year. The team members were Sgt. A. Hawkes, Cpl. C. Ratcliff, Cpl. H. Davis, Tpr. H. Parlour. This competition was run for yeomanry sections from 1873 until 1897 combining the skills of riding and shooting. It was won on this occasion with the remarkable score of 123 points and with a time of 9 minutes 30 seconds. Using the Martini-Henry Carbine, five shots were fired at targets at 500 and 600 yards. The troop leader was Captain H.H. Calvert, who had recently left the 7th Dragoon Guards and the Permanent Staff instructor was RSM H. Hayward.

Major J.E.C. Mathews, 1896. Captain Mathews transferred from the Middlesex Regiment to the RGH in 1893, accepting the rank of Lieutenant in so doing. An artist of considerable ability, he painted for the regiment, *The Blue Duke* and Colonel Bertie Palmer's portrait. Some of his paintings feature in the Royal Collection. He also designed the model for the magnificent silver statuette presented to the 9th Duke of Beaufort by the Regiment on the occasion of his marriage to Baroness Carlo de Tuyll in 1897. He commanded the RGH contingent at Queen Victoria's Diamond Jubilee celebrations which lined part of the route between Whitehall and Buckingham Palace.

The visit of HRH The Prince of Wales to Cheltenham, 13 May 1897. The regiment was encamped for its annual training at this time at Prestbury Park, which is now Cheltenham racecourse. On the left is the Commanding Officer, Colonel the Marquis of Worcester with HRH mounted in the centre. Captain Lionel Barry commanded the regimental escort seen at the rear. HRH had postponed his visit from the year before due to the virulent outbreak of smallpox in the City and suburbs of Gloucester of 1895. The agricultural depression in that year seriously affected the numbers of men able to attend camp.

Sergeant Major H. Brill. In May 1890, permanent duty was held at Cheltenham. During the week a tournament was held in the Montpellier Gardens in which SSM Brill won the tent-pegging competition. He was also a first-class shot. His Long Service and Good Conduct Medal seen on his chest is now displayed in the Regimental Museum.

Farrier Sergeant A. Spreadbury won the 'Best turned-out Man and Horse' prize in 1888. He was the NCO in charge of the Cheltenham contingent at Queen Victoria's Diamond Jubilee celebrations.

Trooper G.S. Turk served for twenty-one years in the Regiment and was finally commissioned into the AOD (Ordnance Corps) in 1915. On mobilization in 1914, he was reported as having been seen at 6 a.m. riding his horse fully equipped to join up at the Regimental HQ in Gloucester.

Cheltenham Troop RGH, 1899. Seated, left to right from fifth on left: Farrier Sgt. Spreadbury, SQM Bastin, Maj. J.E.C. Mathews, Maj. W.H. Wyndham-Quin MP, Lt. E.H. de Freville, Sgt. Major H. Brill.

The Berkeley Troop in May 1898 commanded by Captain W.H. Playne, who later commanded the Regiment at Gallipoli. Mounted drills were often undertaken in Berkeley Deer Park at about this time. Lord Fitzhardinge would come out to spectate and dispense ale and cheese to the yeomen after dismissal.

Corporal H.W. Prout of the
Berkeley Troop, 1898. Howard Prout
was one of thirteen children born
and brought up at Parks Farm,
Frampton-on-Severn where their
father James held the tenancy. The
family still farm nearby.

3rd (Gloucestershire) Coy., 1st Bn. Imperial Yeomanry at Horfield Barracks, Bristol
during training before embarkation for South Africa in January 1900. Note the heavy
web bandoliers which were later replaced by two of leather, one of which was often worn
round the horse's neck.

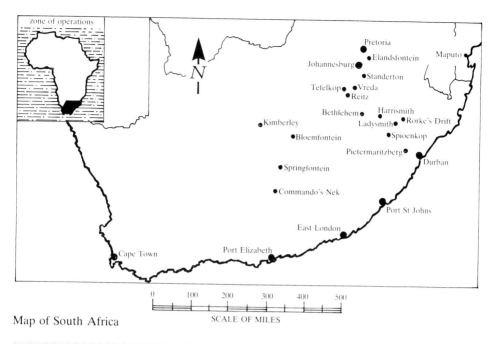

Map of South Africa

SCALE OF MILES

1st Bn. Imperial Yeomanry near Capetown, South Africa, 1900. The 1st and 2nd Coys were from Wiltshire, the 3rd from Gloucestershire and the 4th from Glamorgan. The officers of the Gloucestershire Coy. were: Capt. W.H. Playne (of Longfords House, Avening), Capt. E.T. Hill (late 19th Hussars), Capt. C.G.M. Adam (late 14th Hussars), Capt. A.L. Grahame-Clark (of Frocester Manor), and Lt. the Hon. R.B. Robertson. This was the first time that the yeomanries were sent to serve abroad and the RGH won its first Battle Honour in the campaign against the Boers. Maj. Wyndham-Quin, late Adjutant to the RGH 1889–95, took command of the battalion after the CO was invalided home soon after leaving Maitland Camp, where dysentery and enteric fever were rife. The regiment was to suffer eleven fatal casualties during the war. In his *History of the RGH Yeomanry 1892–1922*, Frank Fox writes: 'Sickness and short rations had played havoc with Captain Playne's troop engaged in holding Commando's Nek, and out of twenty-eight men only fourteen remained, with four English horses. The deficiency in horses was made up with native ponies.'

19

A trooper of 1st Bn. Imperial Yeomanry, 1901. Lines of communication were often very stretched in the closing stages of the Boer War, resulting in considerable lack of uniformity in kit. No regimental badges, shoulder-titles or pugris were worn, thus it is difficult to identify in which company this yeoman served. A newspaper report of 1901 lists the following as the field equipment of a cavalry trooper in South Africa: saddle, wallets and carbine bucket; bridle complete; spare horseshoe and nails in shoecase; lance, carbine and sword; 150 rounds of ammunition; bandolier, mess tin and water bottle; rations for man and horse; great coat, blanket, numnah; forage net, corn sack, etc. All the kit listed was weighed, giving a total of 115 lb; with the average weight of the rider reckoned at 166 lb, the total load for the horse was 281 lb or just over 20 st.

Henry Clifford enlisted into the Imperial Yeomanry in December 1899 and was promoted sergeant to command No. 4 Troop of the Gloucestershire Coy. after the capture of Ladybrand in May 1900. He was later commissioned before the Regiment's return home in July 1901.

Sir Lionel Darell writes in his autobiography *Ratcatcher Baronet*: 'My next-door neighbour in Gloucestershire, Henry Clifford, got married in London to Miss Clay – an important event, in that his tenants and many farmers came up on the early train from home for the "day out"; 7.50 a.m. After the wedding . . . I promised to entertain them at Knightsbridge barracks. The men were all at evening stables, and nothing would do but an exhibition of riding to please these farmers in the riding school, and we all had a jolly half hour there, especially as one old "rustic" remarked that he did not think much of our horsemanship (farmer Coole from Frampton), whereupon he was invited to get up, and dear old Bill Coole was not long before he hit the dust, or rather the tan, and on rising, amid much merriment, demanded yet another drink!'

The citizens of Dursley welcome home one of their local boys from South Africa in July 1901.

Lieutenant-Colonel the Duke of Beaufort ADC TD. 'An event of great interest and importance to the Regiment took place on 14 May, 1900, when it assembled for permanent training at Ross. For the first time in its history the Regiment trained outside the borders of its own county and under canvas, and for twenty-one days instead of seven. This gave the camp the flavour of the "real thing". Temporary stables of wood and canvas were erected for the horses' (Fox). Previously the men had been billetted in local hostelries with their mounts. The 9th Duke commanded the RGH from 1899 until 1904 and then served as Honorary Colonel from 1904 until 1924. An excerpt from *Happy Odyssey*, General Carton de Wiart's autobiography reads: 'During my first winter as Adjutant I had a flat in Cirencester, and after that a house in Brinkworth, on the edge of the Duke of Beaufort's country. The Duke was a wonderful man to hounds and had that enviable knack of always being in the right place at the right moment. The power of anticipation plays an important part in nearly all sport and games, but in hunting and in the MFH it adds enormously to the enjoyment of the entire field. The Duke weighed twenty stone and rode colossal horses. He never jumped a fence but opened a gate with such dexterity that he shot through quicker than anyone else could jump the nearby fence. Later, when he had to give up riding, he hunted in a Ford and still managed always to be on the spot, and he can have had no superior as a fox hunter.'

Lieutenant-Colonel the Duke of Beaufort, Commanding Officer in Badminton Park at camp in May 1902 with the Inspecting Officer General Sir Evelyn Wood VC GCB. Two years later the General decided that the Regiment should train at Cheddar Camp on the Mendips. The Duke disagreed and promptly resigned. He was succeeded by Lieutenant-Colonel Hedley Calvert, who was second-in-command at the time. He had earlier served in the 7th Dragoon Guards as a subaltern. After retiring from the RGH in 1909, he commanded the 3rd line of the Regiment on the outbreak of the First World War. 'The year 1903 was marked by the temporary abolition of the distinctive Badminton blue Hussar uniform except for officers attending levees. The new orders prescribed the regulation Service dress for officers, and the drab Service dress, with blue collars and shoulder straps with the letters RGHIY in brass for the men. The cuffs of the jacket were braided with a blue Austrian knot. Bedford cord breeches with a thin blue welt were worn, black boots, blue puttees, and slouch hats turned up on the left side to show the regimental badge in bronze. The cavalry type of saddlery was continued, the officers' chargers wearing the scarlet plume. The new dress was brought into use gradually, one squadron being fitted out at a time' (Fox).

A Sqn RGH at Cheddar Camp in May 1904. Seated centre: SSM J. Heather, Major Gilbert Henry, Lieutenant. R.C. Forster.

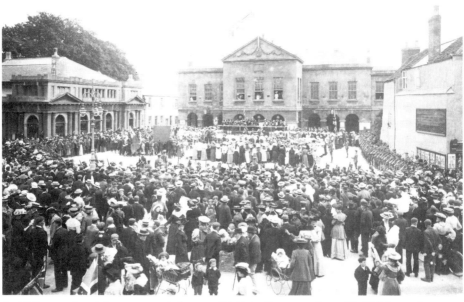

In 1905 annual training was carried out at Wells in Somerset from 10–27 May under ideal weather conditions. The total strength in camp was 365. Empire Day was celebrated on 24 May, when the RGHY lined the town square for the celebrations.

At the County Rifle Meeting held at Bedminster, near Bristol on 7 June 1905 the
Mardon Challenge Cup (value £50) was won on its first presentation by the regimental
team. This competition was open to all units, regular and auxillary, connected with the
county. Mr Mardon, the donor, was a member of the old established printing family in
Bristol. 'At Bisley the regimental team – Lt.-Col. R.P. Sandeman, SSM F.D.W Hunt,
Sgt. P. Hoddell, Tpr. J.L. Bennett – succeeded for the first time in winning the
Yeomanry Inter-Regimental Challenge Cup. Lt.-Col. Sandeman won the St George's
Vase at this meeting' (Fox). Standing, left to right: Trumpeter A.J. Griffin, A Sqn.; Cpl.
J.E. Williams, B Sqn; L-Sgt. A. Butler, B Sqn; Capt. L.E.H.M. Darell (Adt.); Tpr.
F.G. Bell, D Sqn; Tpr. J.L. Bennett, B Sqn; L/Cpl. A.E. Matthews, A Sqn Seated, left
to right: Sgt. P. Hoddell, C Sqn; Sgt. E. Hunt, D Sqn; SSM G. Thorneycroft,
(Permanent Staff), Mr R. Mardon; Lt.-Col. R.P. Sandeman; SSM J. Heather,
(Permanent Staff); SSM F.D.W. Hunt, D Sqn.

D Sqn RGH Imperial Yeomanry at Bristol, 1 April 1906. Inspection by Lieutenant-
General Sir Ian Hamilton, KCB, DSO followed by the Adjutant, Captain Lionel Darell.
Many of the regiment were later to serve under this Inspecting Officer in less auspicious
circumstances on the Gallipoli Peninsula in 1915.

Signallers of the Gloucestershire Yeomanry. 'The year 1907 was a quiet one in the annals of the Regiment, marked by no outstanding events. The ordinary work was carried on with interest and efficiency. Annual training took place at Piercefield Park, Chepstow, Monmouthshire, in the last fortnight of May, and the Regiment encamped for the first time as a cavalry regiment, tents and horse lines together' (Fox). At Bristol on 25 July, the regimental signallers were examined and received a very satisfactory report. This was naturally very gratifying to Captain Darell (seated centre) who during his adjutancy (1904–8) put a great amount of work and enthusiasm into raising the standard of signalling in the regiment. Note the flags for semaphore and the lamps for communicating at night.

Permanent Staff RGH 1908. The regular instructors wore the RGH uniform during their tour with the regiment. Standing, left to right: SSM G. Thorneycroft; SSM W. Gregory, whose DCM was won with the regiment in South Africa. Seated, left to right: RSM J. Heather, Capt. L.E.H.M. Darell, Adjutant; Mr E. Deavin, Bandmaster.

Church Parade of the Territorial Forces of Gloucester and District, 3 May 1908. RGH in three ranks on the right: Lt.-Col. H.H. Calvert at the front with Maj. W.H. Playne on his right. The three Troop Leaders in front of each rank are: Lt. H.F. Clifford (front rank), Lt. J.D. Birchall (middle rank), 2nd Lt. M.G. Lloyd-Baker (rear rank). The Adjutant, Capt. L.E.H.M. Darell is in Life Guards uniform to the rear.

The Oldown Troop outside Oldown House, Tockington, 1908. 2nd Lt. C.E. Turner and 2nd Lt. A.H.S. Howard are seated, with cross-belts. Charles Turner later won the DSO commanding D Sqn at the Battle of Romani. He commanded the Regiment on its return home from Palestine in 1919. Algar Howard of Thornbury Castle won the MC in Palestine. His clear and vivid diaries of life with the RGH in the First World War provided Frank Fox with much of the detail for his regimental history. He became Garter King of Arms in later life.

The Oldown Troop of the RGH Yeomanry entraining at Thornbury station, 1909.

The Oldown Troop detraining at Thornbury station in 1909 on return from exercise.

The Oldown Troop being dismissed by their Troop Leader, Lt. C.E. Turner at the Plain, Thornbury in 1909.

Camp at Sudeley Castle, Winchcombe in May 1908. Staff and NCOs, seated centre row, left to right: Farrier QMS Spreadbury, QMS Davis, RSM Heather, Lt.-Col. Sandeman, Col. Calvert, Capt. Darell, SSM Hayward, -?-. 'The weather was unfavourable; very wet and cold for the first half of the camp. The field selected for the camp was described by a local veteran to be "the wettest in Gloucestershire" and the approach was a veritable sea of mud, but once the main track was crossed it proved an excellent site' (Fox). 2nd Lt. Mickey Hicks Beach (later Lord Quenington) joined the Regiment from 4th Bn. the Gloucestershire Regiment. Not long after he married Miss Dent-Brocklehurst, the squire of Sudeley's daughter. Tragically she died in Egypt, three weeks after her husband was killed at Qatia. Her brother G.E. Dent-Brocklehurst served in 2nd RGH during the First World War.

The band at camp in Badminton Park, 1911, under Bandmaster Mr E. Deavin in a forage cap.

RGHY at Badminton, May 1911, Officers' Mess Group in full dress. Standing, left to right: Lt.-Col. H. Bramwell TD FRCS, 2nd Lt. Hon. M.H. Hicks Beach, 2nd Lt. H.M. Calvert, 2nd Lt. A.W. Clifford, Lt. J.D. Birchall, Lt. C.E. Turner, 2nd Lt. H.B. Gething, 2nd Lt. G.N. Horlick, 2nd Lt. J.T. Colledge, 2nd Lt. A.H.S. Howard, Lt. T.J. Longworth, 2nd Lt. M.A. Sands, 2nd H.G. de Lisle Bush, Revd F. Tower MA. Seated, left to right: Lt. M.G. Lloyd-Baker, Capt. R.C. Forster, Capt. and Adjt. W.E. Lawrence (Royal Scots Greys), Maj. C.G.M. Adam, Lt.-Col. R.P. Sandeman, Col. the Duke of Beaufort TD ADC, Maj. W.H. Playne, Capt. R.M. Yorke, Capt. A.J. Palmer, Capt. H.F. Clifford, 2nd Lt. Hon. H.F. Charteris.

Camp scene at Badminton, 1912; a moment's respite from stable management.

Officers' Servants' Mess Tent at camp in Badminton Park, 1912.

RSM J. Heather at Bulford Camp on
Salisbury Plain, 1913. He was later
commissioned into the Royal Flying
Corps during the First World War.

A lecture in Camp at Bulford in 1913.

Major H.C. Elwes commanding B Sqn in 1913. The squadron at that time consisted of two Cotswold Troops, a Tetbury and a Berkeley Troop.

Major Cecil Elwes MVO of Colesbourne as second-in-command in 1914. He took over command of the Regiment in Gallipoli after Lieutenant Colonel Playne had been seriously wounded in the advance on Chocolate Hill. He was posted to the Western Front from Egypt in the spring of 1916 and was later awarded the DSO on returning to his old regiment, the Scots Guards, in France.

Officers and NCOs of A Sqn RGH during the Brigade Camp at Bulford on Salisbury Plain in May 1913. A Sqn consisted of Tewkesbury, Ledbury, Cheltenham and Gloucester Troops. Standing back row, left to right: four troop sergeants and two corporals. Seated centre row, left to right: SQMS, SSM, 2nd Lt. H.M. Calvert, Maj. W.H. Playne, Capt. M.G. Lloyd-Baker, Lieutenant the Hon. H.F. Charteris, Lt. A.W. Strickland, -?-. Seated front row: four troop corporals with Farrier Sgt. Major in centre. These were many of the dramatis personae three years later at the tragic affair at Qatia. Both Michael Lloyd-Baker and Hugo Charteris (later Lord Elcho) were killed. The latter's brother-in-law Tom Strickland was taken prisoner of war.

RGH Trumpeters, May 1914, at Patcham Camp near Brighton.

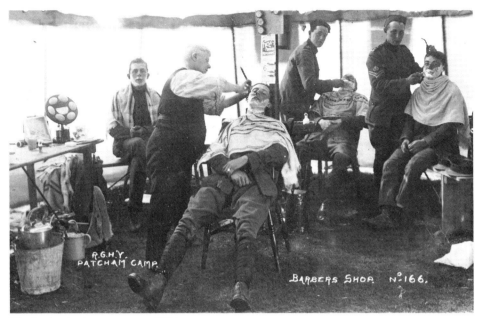

The barber's shop at camp, 1914.

'Following in father's footsteps', a scene from annual camp at Patcham, Sussex in May 1914.

Capt. A. Carton de Wiart, 8th Hussars, Adjutant RGH 1912–14, at Patcham Camp near Brighton in May 1914. He is mounted on the thoroughbred, 'Lie-a-Bed', winner of the Royal Hunt Cup at Ascot the year before. An excerpt from his autobiography reads; 'It was at a shoot in Bohemia with Prince Colloredo that I met Colonel Bob Sandeman. He was the Colonel of the Royal Gloucestershire Hussars, a fine sportsman and a natural soldier, and my delight must have been plainly visible when he offered me his adjutancy. Loath as I was to soldier in England, I knew the life of a yeomanry adjutant was an enviable lot and renownedly pleasant both militarily and socially, and Gloucestershire the heart of good hunting country. In such a county the first things came first and the training of the Yeomanry was most carefully timed not to interfere with the may fly season and to finish before the hunting, but during our weeks of training the enthusiasm and keenness of the officers and men were really stimulating. We put them through a gruelling training and still they asked for more, and would have been extremely disappointed if they had not got it. The nights were hilarious and rowdy and produced the casualties we had not suffered by day.

In the early autumn when there was no training, no fishing and no hunting, I found a delightful system whereby I conducted my adjutancy from the Continent by a correspondence course. I had all the papers sent out to me to sign and return, and occasionally and regretfully resorted to the expense of a wire. All this showed the lack of national crises and high degree of efficiency and smartness of the Royal Gloucestershire Hussars, who were undoubtedly the pick of the Yeomanry and quite capable of entirely running their own show.'

Later he commanded 8th Glosters in France, and it was at La Boiselle that Lt.-Col. de Wiart won his VC and led the 8th Bn. forward to its objective against terrific odds, the only battalion to do so in the brigade. Carton de Wiart held his own ground but in addition, as the one Commanding Officer still in action, rallied the rest of the brigade to hold its ground. He later rose to the rank of general.

Regimental band on sight-seeing trip to Brighton from Patcham Camp in 1914.

Ted Pullin came from Kempley and was a member of the Ledbury Troop.

Trooper Sidney Taylor, also a member of the Ledbury Troop.

Patcham Camp in 1914, 'Corporal of the Feed' on the right. 'In 1906, the system of temporary stables for the horses was abolished and the animals were picketed out, to accustom them to the method of picketing in squadron lines. There had prevailed the idea that the men would not bring out such good horses to training unless provision was made for wooden stabling. It was seen, however, that these stables were draughty and horses consequently suffered from colds. The woodwork of the mangers and supports, being green, after a few days in camp almost disappeared through the horses gnawing it away. Though for a time some still doubted the advisability of putting a valuable hunter on lines in the open, the prejudice was soon overcome by the better health of the animals and the extraordinary improvement in many of the horses at the end of the training period' (Fox).

Camp near the sea, Patcham, May 1914. Under the new Army Orders of 1913, eight motor cyclists were allowed for each regiment. Accordingly, Tprs G.L. Kent and H.L. Whitaker from A Sqn, C.L. Harding from B, M.G. Perkins from C, and G.B. Fry, A. Rowe and J.W. Sandell from D, were appointed as L/Cpl. motor cyclists.

Sergeant Ben James of Great
Norwood Street, Cheltenham.

The Gloucester Troop led by Sergeant Ben James returning to stables down Southgate
Street in August 1914. He is followed by Cpl. C.L. Lane and Cpl. J. Lane of Sandhurst.
Fred Herbert of Matson and George Evans of Staunton are in the rear group.

First month of mobilization in 1914. Recruits parading with their new companions on the Oxleaze outside Gloucester. The cathedral can be seen in the background. 'In September, 1914, orders were received to form a second Regiment of RGH under the command of Lt.-Col. R.P. Sandeman, TD and later on a third Regiment of RGH was formed under the command of Lt.-Col. H.H. Calvert TD' (Fox).

B Sqn Officers' haversack lunch at Churn on the Berkshire Downs near Newbury in September 1914, after the inspection of the 2nd Mounted Division by HM King George V. Left to right: 2nd Lt. John Bengough, 2nd Lt. Frank Mitchell, 2nd Lt. Lord Apsley with bottle, Maj. Henry Clifford, Lt. Lord Quenington, Capt. Tommy Longworth.

2nd RGH Officer's Group, 1914. Left to right: Lt. R.A. Bennett of Marlwood Grange, Thornbury. He was Secretary to the Berkeley Hunt after the war. Maj. A.E. Gibbs served in the 6th Inniskilling Dragoon Guards during the Boer War. Having left the army in 1903, he re-enlisted in the RGH in 1914. He died at Winson Manor, near Cirencester, in 1922. 2nd Lt., the Hon H.W. Ponsonby, later Lord de Mauley, was the first of three generations to serve in the Regiment, and lived at Little Faringdon near Lechlade. 2nd Lt. R.G. Anderson, whose father was agent at Cirencester Park, served with 2nd RGH in England and then with 1st RGH in Palestine. He was killed in the action of Balin near Jerusalem on 12 November 1917. His war diary was lent to Frank Fox by his parents for the writing of the regimental history. He was a talented musician and before the unveiling ceremony of the RGH Memorial in College Green in 1922, an anthem that he composed was played at the Cathedral service.

Machine-gun troop, 1914. Lt. G.N. Horlick of Cowley Manor commanded the machine-gun troop while the Regiment was encamped on Newbury racecourse during the autumn of 1914. They were part of the South Midland Mounted Brigade with the Worcestershire and Warwickshire Yeomanries. Sgt. H.A. Colburn is manning the Maxim machine-gun on the right. He was later to win the Military Medal with A Sqn at Qatia.

2nd Lt. Lord Apsley's Abergavenny Troop, November 1914. Back row, left to right:
Tprs, E. Williams, Hobbs, Godwin, Hiley, Phelps. Standing: Tprs, Kynch, Archibald,
Iles, E. Marsh, J. Williams, W.J. Edwards, Edwards, -?-, Woodward, Anstey, Wright,
Gent and Temlett. Seated: Tpr. Mitchell, Cpl. Orchard, Cpl. Jones, PSI Duxbury, 2nd
Lt. Lord Apsley, SSM Butler, Sgt. Day, SQMS Williams, Tpr. Watkins, Tpr. G.
Edwards. On the ground: Tprs, O'Connell, Baker, Carr, W. Pickering, Mason, J.
Pickering, Bott.

No. 3 Troop D Sqn RGH, 1915, Second Lieutenant the Hon. H.W. Ponsonby's Troop.
D Sqn consisted of three Bristol Troops and the Oldown Troop.

On 17 December 1915 the Duke of Beaufort inspected the Reserve Regiment of the Gloucestershire Yeomanry under the command of Lt.-Col. Bob Sandeman on the Oxleaze at Gloucester. With the Duke were Sir Arthur Anstice and Herbert Lord, Master of the Cotswold Hounds, from Lilleybrooke. The ladies watching the jumping include Miss Lord, Lady Blanche Somerset and Lady Diana Somerset.

Second Lieutenant Ponsonby encouraging a member of his troop, Tpr. Church, down the jumping lane.

Some members of the Ledbury Troop, A Sqn at Hunstanton, December 1914. Seated, left to right: Cpl. Charlie Mayo, Sgt. Harry Walker, Cpl. Horace Smith. Standing: Rodney Powell, Ted Pullin, Reg Shipton, Ted Price, Hubert Meredith, Nat Jenner, Walter White, Nobby Clark. Back row: Bill Morris, Sid Taylor.

2nd RGH Draghounds, Norfolk, 1915. Major Charlie Scott of Buckland Manor, Broadway, was Master of the North Cotswold Hounds in peacetime. He had five couple of hounds sent from Gloucestershire and met once a week, hunting over the Norfolk countryside with enthusiastic support from the local farmers.

Howard Lord of B Sqn, which had one Berkeley Troop at that time. The Lords farmed at Hartsgrove Farm, Wanswell near Berkeley. Tpr. Lord sailed with the Regiment from England on 9 April 1915 and served right through, taking part in the entry into Aleppo, Syria in 1918. His son still runs the Berkeley Arms pub and farms at Purton.

Regimental cooks preparing a meal at Chieveley Camp, near Newbury, in 1914.

SS *Saturnia*. The RGH, three squadrons strong, entrained at Hunstanton on 10 April 1915 for Avonmouth. The next day, with other units of the 1st Mounted Brigade of the 2nd Mounted Yeomanry Division, the Regiment embarked to join the British Mediterranean Force on the transports *Minneapolis* and *Saturnia*. They disembarked at Alexandria in Egypt a fortnight later, under the command of Lt.-Col. Playne, who was later severely wounded at Gallipoli.

Lt.-Col. Bill Playne seen here mounted at Patcham Camp, 1914. He lived at Longfords House which lies beneath Gatcombe. His mill next door, Longfords Mill, produced much famous cloth: red for guardsmen's tunics ('Stroudwater Scarlet'), green for billiard tables and white for tennis balls. The firm was later taken over by Winterbotham and Strachan.

The SS *Minneapolis* at Avonmouth before sailing on 15 April 1915.

Captain Tommy Longworth of Long Newnton was second-in-command of C Sqn and was later badly wounded at Gallipoli. The squadron consisted of the Cardiff, Newport, Abergavenny and Monmouth Troops. The Squadron was broken up on mobilization to reduce the Regiment to a three squadron organization.

On board the *Minneapolis en route* to Egypt. 'The ordered destination of the transports was Malta. On the way was passed the *Wayfarer*, carrying the horses of the Warwickshire Yeomanry, which had been torpedoed by the enemy [in the Bristol Channel]. The other transports were not allowed to stand by for her assistance, but were ordered to make at full speed for the open sea' (Fox). The Warwicks came on without their unfortunate horses.

Kit inspection on board *Minneapolis*. The Regiment arrived at Chatby Camp without having lost a single horse or mule on the journey from England. This showed good horsemastership, and was due also to the splendid way in which those officers and men who were not overcome by seasickness took on the work of less fortunate comrades during the sea voyage. Howard: 'We spent our time in half-hour shifts all day looking after our horses. Few men could stand the horse decks more than half an hour without being sick. All horses were tied up and never moved for three weeks. By dint of much leg massage, and sponging out ears and nostrils we practically lost no horses on the voyage.'

On guard at Chatby Camp. 'On 24 April the RGH disembarked at Alexandria and after spending a night in the streets near the dock, marched into camp at Chatby Beach, near that city. Their first welcome to the East was a severe sand-storm' (Fox).

Bathing at Chatby. 'The horses and mules found the heat of the unsheltered lines at Chatby very severe after the cool breezes of the east coast of England. Their food, considerably changed from what they had been accustomed to, did not help the situation, but by careful and constant attention they kept their condition wonderfully well. Gradually they became acclimatized to withstand the far greater trials which they had to face later in the campaign. Chatby was about the only place where locusts made their appearance in large quantities' (Fox).

David and Algy Byrd at Chatby Camp, outside Alexandria.

A Sqn trumpet practice on the beach at Chatby. Since the Boer War, cavalry trumpeters carried both a bugle and a trumpet. The bugle was for easier use when mounted and moving.

De-lousing at Chatby. 'At Chatby the Regiment was severely tried by an outbreak of what was called "Chatby fever", but which seems to have had its origin, not in Chatby, but in some billets which the men had occupied in England before their departure. The symptoms were somewhat like those of jaundice, and sufferers experienced very high temperatures. The duties of the RGH whilst at Chatby were chiefly in connection with providing guards at various headquarters and camps in and around Alexandria. Squadron drill in rather confined areas took place in the early morning, with musketry exercises and lectures later in the day and bathing for horses and men' (Fox).

Barber's shop, where Trooper Taylor receives a prison crop, one of the best cures for lice.

Alexandria, 26 May 1915. Lt. Algar Howard's diary relates: 'At 4 a.m. we were turned out to quell a riot of Egyptian labour corps, who had refused to go on board ship and had escaped. Charles Turner, self and Tim Cripps and 150 turned out in 5 motor lorries. Went to quay, found they had just escaped into the bourse, (large square in middle of town). We went off again in the five lorries and debouched from five points and completely surrounded them (100 in number) with fixed bayonets. They were armed with iron crow bars but were quickly disarmed and marched back to their boat. As they were still rebellious, a guard of 1 officer and 21 men were put over them to take them to Dardenelles or Lemnos and I got the job. Started on SS *Junin* at 8 p.m.'

Moving the tailor's shop at Chatby.

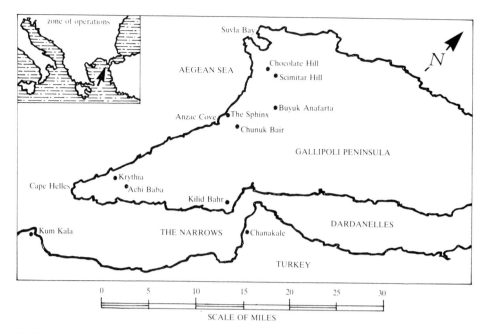

Gallipoli map. 'On 11 August unexpected orders came for the yeomanry to proceed to Gallipoli, dismounted. Each regiment was to leave four officers and 100 OR and all its horses in Egypt' (Fox). SS *Haverford* and SS *Ascania* carried the RGH, less one squadron, to Gallipoli. 'At sea all ranks were inoculated against cholera. That, and the prospect of submarines (the *Royal Edward* had been sunk by a submarine on 14 August), were the only troubles of the voyage, which was favoured by splendid weather' (Fox).

Reluctant Infantryman. 'Infantry web equipment was served out to all ranks. The RGH forgot all regret at thus becoming infantry in delight at the prospect of coming face to face with the enemy and in satisfaction at the remembrance that they had always been famed at home for their musketry, and now there was work to do with the rifle' (Fox).

53

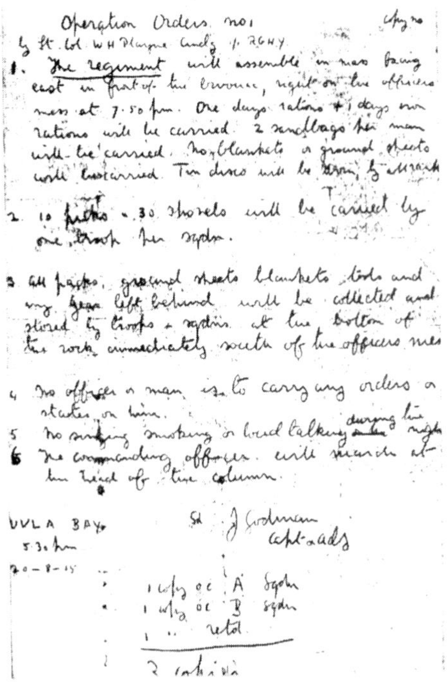

Operation Orders. no 1

[handwritten operation order, largely illegible]

By Lt. Col W H Playne Cmdg p. 26 R.Y

1. The regiment will assemble in mass facing east in front of the bivouac, right on the officers mess at 7.50 pm. One days rations + 3 days own rations will be carried. 2 sandbags per man will be carried. No blankets or ground sheets will be carried. Tin discs will be worn by all ranks.

2. 10 picks + 30 shovels will be carried by one troop per sqdn.

3. All packs, ground sheets blankets, tools and any gear left behind will be collected and stored by troops & sqdns at the bottom of the work immediately south of the officers mess.

4. No officer or man is to carry any orders or states on him.

5. No singing smoking or loud talking during the night.

6. The commanding officer will march at the head of the column.

SUVLA BAY
5.30 h
20-8-15

Sd J Godman
Capt & Adj

1 copy OC A Sqdn
1 copy OC B Sqdn
1 .. retd.
2 retained

Operation Order, Gallipoli, August 1915. The composite Regiment on foot landed at A Beach Suvla Bay in small boats at midnight on 17 August to the sound of 'Gone Away' by a yeomanry officer on his hunting horn. These orders were for the move to Lala Baba Hill, thence to Chocolate Hill where the Regiment took the first of its many casualties. Second Lieutenant Gething and eleven yeomen were killed and the Commanding Officer and nearly fifty yeomen, severely wounded.

Cooks butchering meat at the regimental bivouac on Lala Baba Hill on 21 August before the move to Chocolate Hill. Thence, they lived entirely on bully, biscuit and lime juice except for the sick who lived on Horlick's malted milk.

Yeomen in the firing line, Gallipoli. Note the reluctant infantrymen still wearing their spurs. Extract from an officer's diary for 26 August reads: 'Front line trenches. Digging ammunition trench in moonlight, sniped all the time. Trench very smelly. Four dead Turks found buried in corner. You can't imagine how interesting and beastly it all is. Sniping constantly and bursting of shells. One man dropped his sham teeth in the battle the other day and has had to go to hospital as he cannot bite the biscuit; it is just like dog biscuit.'

Yeomen with camp staff at Mena. On 31 October, the depleted regiment withdrew from the Gallipoli peninsula with a strength of nine officers and eighty-one NCOs and yeomen. In mid-November they embarked from South Pier, Mudros and were lightered on to the transport SS *Themistocles*, which sailed for Alexandria from where they proceeded to rejoin their horses with the rear party at Mena Camp, near Cairo.

Yeomen relaxing on the Pyramids. One squadron was left behind in Egypt during the
Gallipoli Campaign to look after the regiment's horses.

Members of the rear party enjoying a tourist's day out at the Sphinx.

A Squadron at the Pyramids in 1915. The Squadron consisted of troops from Tewkesbury, Ledbury, Cheltenham and Gloucester.

Officers of 2nd RGH in 1915. Back row, left to right: Lt. C.C. Herbert, Lt. H.W. Kemble, Lt. C.T. Scott, 2nd Lt. G.E. Dent-Brocklehurst, 2nd Lt. the Hon. H.W. Ponsonby, -?-, 2nd Lt. R.G. Anderson, 2nd Lt. A.S. Willes, Lt. M.W. Muir, -?-, 2nd Lt. S. Dennis, 2nd Lt. G.V. de Freville. Front row: Lt. H.E. Whitaker-Cantrell, Capt. C.E.F. Henry, Capt. H.W. Dawes, Maj. R.A. Scott, Maj. A.E. Gibbs, Lt.-Col. R.P. Sandeman, Maj. A.H. Butler, Capt. C.J. Ratcliff, Lt. H.M. Calvert, Lt. A.E.W. Guise, Lt. R.A. Bennett.

2nd RGH Troop group pausing from stables duties in Cirencester Park in 1915. The second-line Regiment was formed both to back up the first-line in Egypt and to act as an independent regiment if necessary.

Will Muir of Postlip Hall, Winchcombe was killed hunting after the war when a joint-master of the Cotswold Hunt. He was the father of Kim Muir, who became one of the most successful amateur jockeys of the late 1930s and was killed serving with the 10th Hussars during the Second World War. Until recently there was a race named after him, run at the National Hunt Festival.

Martin Hartigan at a meet of the RGH Draghounds in Norfolk in 1916. He is talking to Sir Anselm Guise's sister Diana who later married Arden Beaman, commander of the RGH Armoured Car Coy. from 1928 until 1930. Hartigan became a well-known and respected trainer after the war. He trained at Middleham. The great Sir Gordon Richards was apprenticed to him at the start of his career as a young jockey.

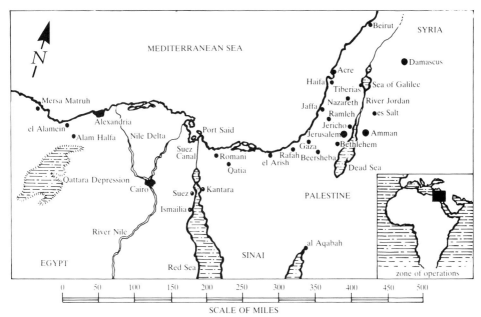

Map of Egypt, Palestine and Syria.

Cpl. Hugh Walwin with 'Black Boy' at Mena Camp, Cairo, in 1915. His photographer's shop still exists in Southgate Street, Gloucester.

61

Lionel Darell

1935:-

Sir Lionel Darell in Life Guards uniform during his year as County High Sheriff in 1924–5 outside Saul Lodge. His father lived at Fretherne Court and served in the RGH in the 1870s. He himself was posted from 1st Life Guards to serve as Adjutant to the RGH from 1904 until 1908. He again served alongside the Regiment as Brigade Major to 1st Mounted Brigade, in which the Regiment was grouped, from 1914 at Warwick until 1916 at Gaza. He wrote interesting accounts of the Regiment in action at Gallipoli and Qatia in his autobiography 'Ratcatcher Baronet'.

Cpl. Hugh Walwin and Sgt. Harry Colburn in Sinai, 1915. Both were wounded and taken prisoner with A Sqn at Qatia the following year.

Sgt. Colburn showing off his equitational skills to the locals in Egypt, 1915. Sgt. Colburn won the MM for gallantry in the action at Qatia. His son became High Sheriff of Gloucestershire in 1980 and his grandson still farms at Northleach.

A photograph of Turkish field kitchens from captured film.

Orderly Corporal inspecting the bread ovens at Mena.

Lt J.C. Bengough of The Ridge, Wotton-under-Edge. He was killed at the action of Agagiya on 26 February 1916 charging the Senussi with the Dorset Yeomanry. At the time he was detached from the RGH as ADC to Major General Peyton who had lent him to the Commanding Officer of the Dorset Yeomanry for this action.

A Turkish-led Senussi force, highly skilled in desert fighting was planning to raid the Nile Delta and British supply bases. Against it stood a composite Imperial force of part-time soldiers going into action for the first time. An attack was launched by the South African Infantry on the Senussi's main position about 15 miles south east of Sidi Barrani. As the enemy withdrew south through the sand hills they were charged from the flank by the Dorset Yeomanry over about 1,000 yards of open ground under heavy fire. The cost was high but the victory was conclusive. Out of a total strength of 84, 5 officers and 27 yeomen were killed and 27 men were wounded; however the result was the complete defeat of the invaders and the capture of their leader, Jaafar Pasha, marking the end of real resistance in the Western Desert.

John Bengough's nephew, Colonel Sir Piers Bengough having served with 10th Hussars, commanded the Royal Hussars 1971/2 and was their Colonel from 1984 to 1990. There is a fox covert in the Berkeley Vale named after the family.

Tack cleaning in the field, Egypt. Left to right: Tprs, Farmer, Pullen, R. Vines, Walwin (holding bit), C. Carter and K. Fowler. Tpr. Vines was wounded at the advance on Chocolate Hill in Gallipoli on 21 August and by Christmas 1915 was commissioned into the Pembrokeshire Yeomanry.

A group of yeomen on a machine-gun course at the Cavalry School at Zeitoun in Cairo. Every British cavalry regiment went to war in 1914 with a detachment of Maxim machine-guns, the standard British machine-gun of the time. These were at first brigaded and then withdrawn to form the Machine Gun Corps.

The butcher's shop in the regimental kitchen at Mena. Left to right: -?-, J. Townsend, J. Lane, L. Vines, Bartlett, -?-, - ?-, -?-, Sgt. C. Smith. Tpr. Lane was later killed in action.

Cpl. Burland Barton in the cook house at Mena. He was later to win the MM and the DCM. 'Wooden huts were erected in Mena Camp and were first used for the Christmas Day dinner in 1915. They were very welcome providing shelter from the glare and heat of the sun' (Fox).

Four yeomen in the Middle-East, back row from left to right: Cpl. Charlie Mayo and Tpr. J.F. Edwards. Front: Cpl. J. Barton and Cpl. Horace Smith. Charlie Mayo, a great character from the Ledbury Troop, was killed in Palestine.

The RGH was the first regiment to cross the Suez Canal in the advance on Palestine.
Here it is seen on its march east from Salhia to Kantara in March 1916.

A Sqn's Ledbury Troop in the Sinai Desert, 1916.

Cpl. Walwin manned A Sqn's only Maxim gun team at The Affair of Qatia on 23 April 1916. He was wounded but kept the gun firing for 7 hours until the bitter end, when it jammed because the water in its water jacket had all evaporated. It was not until four days later, that men of the Australian Light Horse were sent back to the scene of the battle and found two wounded yeomen still alive, Sgt. Charles Lovell (with two bullet wounds and one bayonet wound) and Tpr. O. Scorgie (Lord Elcho's soldier servant). They had both been stripped of all clothes except breeches and left lying in the sun. Local Bedouin had twice tried to throttle Lovell with a telephone wire but it broke. Hugh Walwin and sixty-two others were taken prisoner by the overwhelming Turkish force and thus began a terrible march across the Sinai Desert to Jerusalem and on to Damascus.

Lieutenant Lord Elcho of Stanway had recently given up command of his Winchcombe Troop, when killed in action serving as A Sqn's second in command at Qatia.

Sergeant George Hyatt from Sevenhampton near Andoversford, later A Sqn Sergeant Major, when taken prisoner by the Turks at Qatia. He relates in the Wemyss' family record that the Turks were thunderstruck to find such a small body of men keeping back overwhelming odds for so long.

69

Captain Michael Lloyd-Baker (A Sqn Leader) of Hardwicke and Lieutenant Lord Quenington (Adjutant) of Williamstrip, were both killed on Easter Day 1916 at Qatia. Sometime later on 5 October 1918 after the capture of Damascus and a couple of day's most welcome rest the RGH advanced as leading regiment of the 13th Brigade for the march on Khan Meizelun, a distance of twenty-five miles. The objective was reached in the afternoon and lines were put down on the west side of the village. There was made a curious find. A sword was picked up by one of the Regiment and recognized as that of Captain Lloyd-Baker. It had evidently been taken by a Turkish officer off the field of battle and then abandoned in the retreat north, two years later.

Lieutenant A.W. Strickland was a banker and lived on his family estate at Apperley near Tewkesbury. In 1915, he married Lady Mary Charteris, Lord Elcho's sister. She managed to get herself posted as a nurse to Egypt and sailed out to Alexandria for the wedding but the ship was torpedoed off Port Said and she lost her entire trousseau! She and her sister-in-law became VADs in the Deaconess Hospital in Alexandria which was filled with casualties from Gallipoli. Tom Strickland wrote a vivid account of the Battle of Qatia, from which he was one of two officers to survive as prisoners of war. He died of tuberculosis in 1938. Lady Mary lived on at Apperley Court until her death in 1991.

The problems of maintaining and cleaning a machine-gun in desert conditions in the Sinai. Note the tripod mounting of the Maxim.

Machine-gun training at Romani. Lieutenant the Hon. Elydir Herbert (left) and Lieutenant Gerry Horlick. The latter remained at Kantara in July 1916 to reform A Sqn after the tragedy of Qatia, while the regiment pushed eastwards. Gerry Horlick provided his family's famous malted milk for the yeomen in the Gallipoli trenches, which was a great aid to the many suffering from dysentery. He died of malaria in July 1918 in Alexandria and his parents restored the organ loft in Gloucester Cathedral in his memory.

Qatia, 6 August 1916. After the Battle of Romani, the 5th Mounted Brigade including the RGH took up the pursuit of the Turks alongside the Anzacs back to Qatia. After an initially unsuccessful cavalry attack, the RGH had the satisfaction of re-occupying A Sqn's old position.

A troop pausing in an oasis during a reconnaissance patrol from Romani.

Bathing in the Mediterranean during a spell out of the firing line. The group includes,
Sgt. Mullaney, Tpr. I. Bowen, Cpl. Barton. Tpr. Bowen had been wounded at Chocolate
Hill the year before.

The Battle of Romani, 4 August 1916. Good fortune had placed the RGH on this day at the crucial point of the battle. The following events made up a memorable victory: firstly the iniative of Major Charles Turner in deploying D Sqn into a dangerous gap (for which he was awarded the DSO); secondly the CO Ralph Yorke's dashing charge with two RGH squadrons which took the Turkish-held ridge on Royston Hill; thirdly the engagement and capture of a battery of Turkish camel guns by B Sqn under Lt. Frank Mitchell (for which he was awarded the MC). Frank Mitchell lived at Doughton near Tetbury. He later commanded the RGH Armoured Car Coy. 1931–5. His son served in 11th Hussars and the Regiment after the Second World War.

This scene shows yeomen cleaning their Maxim gun during the operations at Romani in August 1916. These machine-guns were carried on horse-drawn limbers unlike the Hotchkiss guns which replaced the Maxim the following year and were carried on horse back.

A yeoman guarding Turkish prisoners of war after the Battle of Romani. The Regiment had captured 500 prisoners, 4 camel guns and 2 machine guns, suffering only 13 casualties.

Duke of Beaufort's hunt servants between the wars. On the left is George Castle of
Malmesbury (first whipper-in), with Tom Newman (huntsman) and Fred Brown (second
whipper-in). On the outbreak of war in 1914 George Castle left his job of second
whipper-in and enlisted in the RGH. He served in Gallipoli and as a lance corporal won
the MM at Qatia for the gallant rescue of the wounded Lord Quenington, the Adjutant.
Under fire he picked him up and rode with him across his saddle for six miles to safety.
Sadly, the Adjutant had been mortally wounded. As a sergeant he later won the DCM
for charging a machine-gun post that was holding up the Regiment's advance on Nazareth
in 1918. The RGH Hounds in Palestine consisted of one couple known as 'Tripe' and
'Onions'. During a day's hunting in the Gaza area a jackal went to ground. In the
absence of terriers Corporal Castle got into the earth but the sand roof fell in and buried
him. Fortunately his companions were able to dig him out none the worse! He returned
to hunt service in 1919 as first whipper-in at Badminton until his retirement from the
saddle in 1935.

A local Bedouin mother and child with attentive yeomen.

A brief respite from palm branch cutting at Nabit, Sinai, in September 1916.

Camels bringing in palm branches at Nabit. 'Tents were not allowed on account of the activities of hostile aeroplanes, and the men made themselves palm shelters. The Regiment was stationed at Nabit for sometime, doing desert patrol and reconnaissance work from that centre. The horses were on lines in the hod (a grove of date palms), and on a sloping sand dune facing it the officers built themselves huts made of palm leaves. The regimental mess was a great success, until one night, enjoying the best the Regiment could get in this far-away spot, it rained heavily and the meal had to be finished outside. Palm leaves may give protection from sun but they are not recommended when it rains' (Fox).

The Officers' Mess at Nabit. Major Henry Clifford is on the left and Major Bertie Palmer on the right.

Weapon cleaning outside palm shacks. 'Brackish water can generally be found below the surface of the ground at a depth of about 10 feet. This water is usually good enough for horses but not good for human beings. Sometimes it is too salt for horses' (Fox).

Nabit was quite an attractive hod, and the dates were just ripe enough for consumption.

Watering the horses. Note the hogged manes and fly fringes. 'Previously-held ideas as to the capacity of horses to withstand thirst had to be revised in the light of the experience of this campaign, when horses frequently went for two whole days without water and yet survived. The men, who had to face the most serious hardships themselves, did their best throughout for the horses, cheerfully sacrificing their own rest in the effort to secure a drink for their mounts. It was no mean test of discipline and devotion to duty for men who had been fighting all day to devote the whole of the night to getting water for the horses. Many of the men could not prevent going to sleep on horseback while on the march, but this probably enabled them to carry on' (Fox).

Sergeant Frank Barton was the son of 'Judge' Barton, a master blacksmith with a forge at Slimbridge. Frank was one of six boys and seven girls. Two of his brothers, Morris and Burland, also joined up in the RGH in 1915, Frank having already spent his 21st birthday with the IY in South Africa.

In the 1930s and '40s, Frank Barton ran a milk round in the Dursley area. He was a familiar sight in his pony and trap setting out from his Tilsdown home. He was still following the Berkeley Hounds on a horse up to his death in his eighties.

On the march along the Old Roman Road just north of Bir-el-Abd.

Christmas Day service at Malhia, 1916.

Cpl. Jack Walker washing. He was later killed in action.

The much air-raided camp at el Arish. 'On 11 January our camp at el Arish was extended so as to give more space between squadrons. All formations, too, were ordered to construct deep dug-outs in the sand – a difficult order to obey, as there was little or no timber for revetting and the sand was very loose. Enemy aircraft were very active, and precautions had also to be taken against enemy submarines shelling the camp from the sea' (Fox).

'Before the Battle.' The raid on Rafah, 9 January 1917. Commanding Officer's recce party. Major Henry Clifford (second in command) with a telescope in the foreground, was later killed in the action. Lieutenant General Sir Philip Chetwode commanded the recently formed Desert Column, which consisted of the 5th Mounted Brigade (including the RGH), the Anzac Mounted Division, the Imperial Camel Corps, and a battery of HAC, some five thousand in number. His plan was for a mounted raid in strength against a two thousand strong dug-in Turkish position about thirty miles distant from our base at El Arish. After ten hours fighting, the attack was completely successful as practically the whole Turkish force was destroyed. Rafah is now in the Gaza Strip.

Number One Gun in action at Rafah. Thirty thousand rounds were fired by this Maxim at one of the Turkish redoubts at 1,800 yds range, covering the advance of A Sqn.

Number Two Gun at Rafah. Captain the Hon. E.J.B. Herbert, the machine-gun officer is seated centre observing the effect of the Maxim fire on the Turkish redoubt. 2nd Lt. A.C. Byard is seated left. He had been commissioned from the ranks in November 1915 into the third line of the Regiment, but had returned to the first line nine months later.

In camp at Khan Yunus. The Regiment were bivouacked here between the Battles for Gaza. Trooper Welland is wearing an Anzac hat and Lance-Corporal W. Rickards carries a revolver.

The Oldown Troop holding an advanced line in a hastily dug trench at el Munkheileh after the Battle of Attawineh, 19 April 1917. This was during the second Battle of Gaza.

Camels watering at Bayud, September 1916. This shows a typical hod with date palms around a well, which were to be so vital in watering the horses during cavalry actions in Palestine.

Hotchkiss gun team, Palestine, 1917. There was often difficulty experienced in keeping
these guns in action, owing to the percussion caps being separated from the cartridges in
extraction leading to jams. 'The small percussion caps were very difficult to detect in the
bad light, though such jams can be easily remedied by daylight. Several instances
occurred where time was lost owing to the percussion caps getting into the runners and
other mechanisms of the gun' (Fox).

Men of a Hotchkiss gun team of the RGH swimming in the Mediterranean off the beach
at Tel el Marakeb in July 1917. This is now in the Gaza Strip.

Firing at enemy aircraft during the Battle of Gaza. 'Enemy aircraft were constantly busy, emboldened by the fact that our Air Force was very weak in strength and still weaker in regard to the quality of its machines. Indeed, on the position as regards *materiel* we had no warrant to contest the air at all at this stage, and it was only the self-sacrificing gallantry of our airmen which sent them, on their much inferior machines, to meet the Fokkers and Taubes of the enemy' (Fox).

While in the support line in the Jordan Valley the regiment found daily, one patrol troop and one squadron to act against enemy aircraft. Tpr. Perkins on the gun, Tpr. A.D. Townsend feeding the belt and Tpr. London with the range finder.

A morale-boosting arrival of mail for members of the regiment in the Romani area of Sinai late in the summer of 1916.

On 28 July 1917, the Regiment held a sports meeting, which was keenly enjoyed by all ranks. The band and pipers of the 52nd Division helped brighten up the day. The events included wrestling on horseback, a Victoria Cross race, a mounted tug-of-war, a mule race for officers and a harem race.

The harem race at the Regiment sports in 1917.

Yeomen washing their clothes while at Mazoon.

A pause to relax on the machine-gun limbers on the march in the Gaza area.

Troop horses being fed during a temporary halt before the Battle of Beersheba. The chief prize for the capture of this large, squalid Arab village was its excellent water supply. As it lay in the midst of a very arid region, the capture of the wells intact was the lynchpin of Allenby's plan for the start of the Desert Mounted Corps' push north. 'On 5 November the Regiment had a welcome day's rest at Beersheba. The horses had been without water for 48 hours, and the men had been for the same time either fighting or in the saddle. The famished horses on scenting the water could not be restrained, but made a rush for the troughs, and some of the men were also suffering severely from thirst' (Fox).

The ambush party, October 1917, Lt. Robert Wilson, seated centre (author of the recent *Palestine 1917*) led this fighting patrol to Hill 720 near Gaza. For this action he received the MC; his troop sergeant, Sgt. Burland Barton, and Troop Corporal Lane were both awarded the MM. Burland Barton is standing behind his troop leader.

The grave of Trooper. A.E. Wiltshire of D Sqn at Balin. Accurate compass bearings were taken by the burial parties of men who fell on the field of battle so that the bodies could be recovered later for reburial in cemeteries.

After the charge at Huj, 8 November 1917. Two squadrons of Worcestershire Yeomanry and one of Warwicks were in the advance line with the RGH in reserve. A splendid charge with the sword carried the Turkish batteries and routed the infantry protecting the guns. The batteries were manned by German and Austrian gunners, who fought with courage around their guns even after the Turkish infantry had retreated. Twelve guns in all were captured, three of them 5.9 howitzers and nine field guns. The Turks drew their heavy guns with oxen, which supplemented the meagre rations when captured.

Captain the Hon. Elidyr Herbert's section of RGH machine-guns prevented a Turkish counterattack at Huj by capturing the enemy's machine-guns and turning them on to the Turkish infantry as they were recovering from the first shock of the cavalry charge. Captain Herbert was killed four days later at Balin. Men of the RGH are shown around one of the captured Krupp guns.

Major-General Shea commanding the Australian Mounted Division in which the RGH served as part of the 5th Mounted Brigade, receiving the surrender of Jerusalem. Note the escorting yeomen on the left.

General Allenby entering Jerusalem in December 1917. 'On 11 December the Commander-in-Chief, followed by representatives of the Allies, made a formal entry into Jerusalem. He went on foot, with no trappings of State, as a humble palmer rather than a conqueror. In striking contrast was his entry to that, a few years before, of the then Kaiser of Germany with melodramatic pomp which made most of the Christian world inclined either to sorrow or to scoff. The historic Jaffa Gate was opened after years of disuse for General Allenby, and he was thus enabled to pass into the Holy City without making use of the gap in the wall made for the German Kaiser in 1898. By this entry of General Allenby into Jerusalem an old Arab prophecy was fulfilled which said that when the Nile had flowed into Palestine (as it did through our pipe line!) the prophet (Al Nebi) from the west should drive the Turk from Jerusalem' (Fox).

95

2nd RGH, Norfolk, 1916. Fred Winterbotham, of the well-known local family firm of woollen manufacturers Winterbotham, Strachan & Playne from the Stroud valleys, wrote of his days in the yeomanry in his book *The Ultra Spy* (published 1989). He joined up as a 17 year old in 1915 into the second line of the RGH. They were mainly employed in Home Defence and in providing drafts of reinforcements for the first line in Palestine. He writes: 'The summer of 1916 was wearing on; we were wondering where we should go next. Then the blow fell. Cavalry were no longer needed; the brigade would be disbanded into bicycle regiments. Bicycles! Gloom spread to near panic. It affected us all. Bicycles, we knew, were just a step down towards the infantry. Soon there was a call for volunteers for infantry regiments. They were not taken up. Never have I seen hundreds of tough, grown men unashamedly crying as when we loaded our precious horses once more into cattle trucks at the town of Wells in Norfolk. Our horses were our friends and companions, and I think we had all got to love them during the previous eighteen months. Neighing to their masters, they were now going goodness knows where. It was difficult to keep the men from going wild that night in camp.' Note the bicycles on the extreme right.

Captain the Hon. H.W. Ponsonby in France in 1918 when he was acting as ADC to the GOC 15th Army Corps, Lieutenant General Sir John du Cane.

A photograph taken by the Queen of the Belgians on the beach at La Panne in 1917. Left to right: Captain the Hon. H.W. Ponsonby, L/Cpl. Clarke, Tpr. Busby and Tpr Foote, Lt.-Gen. Sir John du Cane. The escort are all from the Wiltshire Yeomanry. It was from this beach adjacent to Dunkirk that thousands of British troops were evacuated twenty-three years later.

Latron, 25 April 1918. Indian transport troops removing RGH tentage by camel. Latron is the southern entrance to the passes through the Judaen Hills, by which the Regiment then passed to the Jordan valley via the familiar Biblical places of Calvary, the Mount of Olives, the Garden of Gethsemane, eventually plunging down the old Roman road into the valley of the Dead Sea. Though it was yet early in the year this valley already gave a hint of the furnace heat which makes it one of the most desolate spots on earth.

Some of the Indian camel troops enjoying a smoke break near Latron.

'Black Boy' and Cpl. Walwin. In 1918, the British Government tragically sold some twenty thousand cavalry horses, to buyers in the Middle East. In 1930, Mrs Dorothy Brooke, whose husband Major-General Geoffrey Brooke was GOC in Egypt at the time, was so shocked by the condition of the surviving horses she saw working in the streets of Cairo (see below), that she set about buying back the remaining five thousand ex-troop horses. It took her four years using funds raised in England. The vast majority, being more than twenty years old and often in the final stages of collapse, had to be destroyed. However, the rest ended their days peacefully amid the care and attention to which they were all once accustomed. Mrs Brooke had founded the Old War Horse Memorial Hospital, later to become the Brooke Hospital for Animals in Cairo that is still flourishing fifty years later.

An overloaded refuse cart in Chatby Camp in 1915.

13th Cavalry Brigade, 1918. Gloucestershire yeomen with members of the Indian Cavalry somewhere in the Jordan Valley near Jericho. In the spring of 1918 Germany concentrated practically her whole strength on the Western Front, as she no longer had to meet the Russian armies. Repercussions of these events in France affected General Allenby's forces considerably. He was called upon during April and May to sacrifice many of his veteran troops to reinforce the French front and to fill their places with Indian troops. This reorganization meant that the RGH found themselves grouped in the 13th Cavalry Brigade with 9th Hodson's Horse and 18th Bengal Lancers, two fully trained regular Indian cavalry regiments, who proved worthy comrades in arms, and with whom they stayed until the end of the war.

29 April 1918 is a date which the Regiment should always keep in its memory – the day they crossed the River Jordan via one of the three pontoon bridges at the Goraniyeah Bridgehead. Lieutenant Colonel A.J. Palmer is on the left. The occupation of the Jordan Valley, besides securing Allenby's right flank, was a necessary first move of any attack on the Hedjaz Railway (see Lawrence of Arabia). It would also cut the Turkish supply line by boat across the Dead Sea from the grain-bearing districts around Kerak. Most vitally it would be a diversion that would draw Turkish troops from the flat coastal plain in the east, where he intended his main strike to be.

The road between es Salt and the el Howeij Bridge, along which the regiment withdrew after one of the strategic cavalry raids into the hills of Moab. Sergeant Insoll of D Sqn won the MM here when with a troop of ten yeomen and one Hotchkiss gun he held an observation post overlooking the bridge. He was attacked by a force of about thirty enemy infantry. He handled his troop with great courage and skill, inflicting severe casualties on the enemy and withdrawing with only one wounded.

Watering horses in the Wadi Auja during the RGH's summer in the Valley of Death. Sir Algar Howard records life in the Jordan Valley: '1,200 ft below sea level, usually 120° F in the shade, the Judaen Hills towering over you in the west and the Moabite Hills to the east. . . . The Jordan was muddy, salt and much too rapid to swim in.' The official military handbook of the day recorded the Jordan Valley as impossible for white occupation during the summer. The agonies of awful heat and blinding sun were shared with scorpions, tarantulas, centipedes and snakes, and appalling white dust. Nor was it the case that the troops had merely to stay there. They had to work – the harsh unremitting labour of trench digging, patrolling, horse care, constant watch for the enemy and also some fighting. That they went through with all this to the triumphant end was the greatest achievement in courage, discipline and endurance of the whole campaign.

The Battle of Megiddo. On 19 September 1918, the Regiment was in the vanguard of Allenby's great breakthrough, with the enemy's GHQ at Nazareth (about fifty miles away) as their first objective. At this time, the Turks were concentrated around the ruined fortress city of Megiddo (or Armageddon) in the midst of the Plain of Esdraelon. The Allied Forces, who had returned Jerusalem to Christian control, were facing the Yilderim and it seemed to many as if this really would be the last great battle of the world as prophesied in the Book of Revelation. In five weeks, the Desert Mounted Corps covered three hundred miles to Aleppo in an astonishing and overwhelming mobile victory, especially when compared to the stalemate in France. In the picture, left to right, are Cpl. Perkins, Tpr. Tripp and Sgt. Marfell in their bivouac.

Cpl. Perkins guarding a captured Bedouin. Nazareth was taken completely by surprise by the regiment, but the enemy GOC General Liman von Sanders managed to evade capture by a hair's breadth. Both Sgts Akers and Wiseman won their DCMs during this action as did the redoubtable Tpr. Forrest whose citation reads: 'This OR when on patrol on 19 September, 1918, noticed a column of waggons moving north from Nahr-el-Falik. He at once galloped at the column with drawn sword and captured the entire column, consisting of 36 waggons, 4 officers and 100 men. Tpr. Forrest, acting on his own initiative, showed great pluck in charging single handed what turned out to be an ammunition column' (Fox).

Captain Lord Apsley was awarded the DSO on 30 September 1918 for his attempt to capture the Austrian wireless station at Kadem. W.T. Massey recorded this exploit: 'An admirable effort was made to secure the German wireless installation. It was a high-powered plant, and by its means the Germans were in constant communication with Constantinople and Berlin. A great deal of German propaganda in the East has passed through this station, and we should have liked to capture it intact. Captain Lord Apsley was sent on a special mission to secure it. He took with him two troops of the Royal Gloucester Hussars Yeomanry, and, leaving after the 14th Cavalry Brigade started for the Kiswe road, they arrived at Kadem station at 4.30. The wireless station was close by, but the German operators had taken no risks. They had prepared the whole equipment for demolition, and on the Gloucesters' approach the great standards were blown up, and a party of Germans and Turks were seen completing the destruction. The Gloucesters charged this party in the hope of saving some of the apparatus, and three Germans and seven Turks were killed with the sword. The remainder surrendered, but before they could be marched away they were reinforced by a considerable number of Germans, and the two troops had to withdraw by a different route from that which they had taken to enter the military area of Damascus. They joined the Australian Mounted Division in the evening. If the two troops had been two divisions they could not have prevented the wreckage of the whole plant, and the Gloucesters' fine action deserved better luck.'

After the capture of Aleppo in October 1918, the Regiment was encamped beneath the walls of this ancient city. Thirty-one officers and men of the RGH who had originally mobilized with the regiment back in the autumn of 1914 took part in the entry into Aleppo. 'The capture of Aleppo had been always a darling object of the Supreme War Council, as it was a strategic centre of the Turkish Empire in Asia. In the old days, before the Cape route to India was developed, Aleppo was the chief trading centre on the road to India, and had close connections with Venice in the palmy days of the Adriatic Republic. Aleppo fell into the hands of the Saracens in the seventh century, was sacked by Tamerlane in the fifteenth century, and was then never occupied by a Western European power until the arrival of the 5th Division in 1918' (Fox). On 19 November, near Aleppo the Regiment gave a hearty welcome to nine of its A Sqn members who had been captured at Qatia in 1915 and now arrived as released prisoners of war from Turkey. These men were entertained at dinner on 21 November. It has to be said to the credit of the Turkish army that these men rejoined their regiment in good condition and apparently had not suffered any severe hardships.

Opposite, top:
Both these yeomen seen here preparing the horses' feeds were among 163 commissioned from the ranks of the Regiment during the First World War, Trooper A.C. Byard (left) into the RGH and Trooper W.B. Cornock (right) into the 3rd Glosters. Sir Algar Howard's diary for October 1918 records: 'During the march from Khan Meizelun to Aleppo we fed entirely on the country except for sugar, milk and bacon which we got where we could. The method was this: before starting, a party of about six men went in advance with the supply officer, who had to requisition mutton or beef, barley and wood, at or near each camp. The sheep were driven in, killed, and butchered, and, if we had time, we always boiled the mutton overnight and ate it cold the next day, otherwise each man had to fry his own. On arrival in camp 75 per cent of the men had to go off with sacks and blankets to fetch barley for the horses; others were sent to gather green millet stalks; and others to forage for wood, to obtain which was always the greatest difficulty. We often had to pull down doors and windows of houses to get enough to do our cooking. After a 15- or 18-mile trek the real day's work was only begun, and everybody was busily engaged up to dark. Hardly a horse was ever groomed. Each regiment took it in turn to do advance guard and outposts for the night.'

During the campaign the horses had performed magnificently, but the experience of feeding them on a ration of a mere 9½ lb of grain a day, combined with watering once in every thirty-six hours (sometimes up to seventy-two hours) had been a great strain. The horses carried two full nosebags and 9 lb of barley in wallets, also two blankets, a greatcoat, a bivouac sheet, sword, rifle, water bucket, shoe case, picketing ropes, etc., making in all at least 18 stone for them to carry.

Return from Palestine, 15 August 1919. The RGH cadre was met by the band and a hero's welcome at the station in Gloucester. They were led by Lieutenant Colonel Charles Turner.

On their return from Palestine, they marched in procession, led by the band to the Saracen's Head Hotel, where they were entertained to luncheon. This pub was in Eastgate Street and has been rebuilt since the war. The photograph shows: Lt.-Col. C.E. Turner DSO TD (centre seated) with Capt. E. Lawrence (Norfolk), Lt. F.C. Brain (Fossebridge), Lt. G.D. Townsend (Cirencester), Lt. G.A. Austell (Cheshire), Lt. R.J.N. Moore (Dorset). Flanked by Sgts V.W. George (Bristol) and P.J. Palmer (Gloucester). The NCOs and yeomen standing include: Tpr. E.J. Pullen and Tpr. G.E. Howell (both of Bristol), Tpr. C.H. Curtis (Bath), Tpr. F. Dickins (Pushdon, Northants), Tpr. R.W. Farnston (Rugby), Tpr. J. Goss (Redhill, Surrey), Tpr. A.J. Kerwood (Lydney), Tpr. F. Wellington (Gloucester), Tpr. W.G. Vren (Liverpool), Sig. A.E. Moore (Bristol), Tpr. S.A .Coggins (London), Tpr. H.N. Petty (Bristol), Cpl. H. Sibley (Birmingham), L/Cpl. S. Coldrick (Bream), Tpr. W. Aspey (Malvern), Tpr. F.E. Pynnan (Bristol).

Lionel Edwards' watercolour of two Dukes of Beaufort, who both at some time were Honorary Colonels of the RGH, 1904–84. The 9th Duke, or 'the Old Duke' as he was affectionately called, is seen in his Ford motor car complete with spade, shovel and terrier. The Marquis of Worcester, later the 10th Duke, is hunting hounds.

There has been a long tradition of fox hunting in the RGH both as an equestrian sport and as a valuable training exercise for cavalrymen. Early in 1890 a regimental call was adopted for which the first bars of the old hunting song 'Do ye ken John Peel?' were not inappropriately selected considering that there were four Masters of Hounds and a Field Master at that time serving in the RGH, and a large number of men, both officers and yeomen, were regular members in the hunting field. The four were Lord FitzHardinge, Lord Worcester, Lord Dangan, Capt. T. Butt-Miller and The Hon. Elton Gifford. One couple of hounds, 'Tripe' and 'Onions', made up the RGH Pack in Palestine and Syria where they hunted the jackal. Later Lt.-Col. Elwes had his own pack of hounds kennelled at Leckhampton, hunting the Kingscote country before the First World War. After the War they were kennelled at Colesbourne when he hunted his own estate in the Cotswold country. Will Muir was killed while hunting with the Cotswold in the 1920s as a joint master. Lord Leigh and Capt. Trevor Smail, successively serving as adjutants from 11th Hussars, hunted the Kingscote Hounds kennelled at Uley during the 1930s with John Talbot whipping in. Lt.-Col. Turner did several seasons as a joint master of the Berkeley after returning from Palestine, 1928–39. Lord Ashton of Hyde was a master of the Heythrop for many years before and after the Second World War and D.E.C. Price, having been a master of the 'Black and Tans', took the VWH (Cricklade) from 1938–41. Capt. Ronnie Wallace, 1st RGH during the Second World War, hunted the Ludlow and both the Cotswold and Heythrop in Gloucestershire and is still hunting hounds on Exmoor. More recently Lt. Simon Hart has hunted the RAC Beagles and the South Pembrokeshire Foxhounds as a serving yeoman.

Colonel C.E. Turner CBE DSO TD at
Berkeley Show in 1952. An extract from
his obituary reads: 'Charles Turner was
not only a great English gentleman and a
magnificent leader but he was much
beloved by all those who came in contact
with him. His interest in the Regiment
and the Old Comrades remained to the
last; hardly any regimental function took
place without his attending it and it was
often he who was responsible for the
success of those gatherings. He was
always at his best at some social function
and how he loved a party!'

Qatia Veterans gather on a visit to Yeomanry Camp at Wheatley Down near Oxford in
1931. Standing, left to right: George Hyatt, Charles Lovell, F. Dilloway, E.J. Tippetts.
Seated: Ben James, Percy Millard, J. Burroughs.

Winchcombe, 1908. Left to right: Tprs Fred Morgan, Herbert Chamberlayne, Frank
Chamberlayne and George Stone.

Together again after 54 years, 1962.

This meet of the Christ Church Beagles on 21 January 1921 was at Fairford Park, the home of the Commanding Officer Lieutenant Colonel Bertie Palmer. After six years of war, many of the yeomen who had joined straight from school, resumed their educational careers in 1920. Both Lord Apsley and Fred Winterbotham found themselves at Oxford with Chetty Hilton-Green, who was hunting the beagles and who himself joined the RGH until conversion to 21st Armoured Car Coy.

Fairford Park. Aubrey Wykeham-Musgrave MC (earlier Adjutant in Palestine), Lord Apsley, Colonel Bertie Palmer, Mrs Scott, Chetty Hilton-Green and Mrs Palmer at the meet of the Christ Church Beagles. The town hall in the middle of Fairford dated 1936 is named after Colonel Palmer.

Lord Apsley became an intrepid flier while serving with the RGH between the wars. He is seen above with an airman and locals in Mesopotamia in front of a Vernon bi-plane in 1922. In October 1941, he flew himself out to Alexandria to see 2nd RGH off into the desert in their newly-acquired Crusader tanks. He was later killed flying home to England.

HRH The Prince of Wales inspecting the regiment at Wilton House, Wilton, Salisbury in 1923. Regimental officers in the photograph are, from left to right: Maj. F.A. Mitchell, Lt.-Col. and QM S.W. Adderley, Lt.-Col. C.E. Turner, Lt. J. St C Harvey. Among the OR's present are Tpr Fear and L/Cpl. Ivor Fear behind Lt.-Col. Adderley and Cpl. George Fear at the end of the front row. Tpr. Norcott is at the extreme right front.

A Sqn group with Captain Lord Apsley seated centre. A fine illustration of the solid tyred Peerless armoured cars with which the Regiment was equipped when first mechanized, until replaced by Rolls Royce armoured cars in 1928–9.

RGH Rugby Football Team 1924–5 at Gloucester Barracks.

The string section of the RGH band somewhere in England in the mid-1920s.
Bandmaster D. Dawes led the band well into the 1930s.

Peerless armoured cars sheeted down after 'Stables' at annual camp somewhere in
England in the 1920s.

RGH Peerless armoured car, *c.* 1924.

Volunteers from D Sqn RGH who were enlisted into the Regular Army (Royal Tank Corps) for the duration of the General Strike from 7–16 May 1926. A further forty-one volunteers were enlisted at Gloucester and the party proceeded to Bovington Camp under Captain Pedder, the Adjutant.

A group of RGH officers in front of a Peerless armoured car in the early twenties. Left to right: 2nd Lt. G.J. Yorke, Lt.-Col. and QM S.W. Adderley, Maj. A.H.S. Howard, Lt.-Col. C.E. Turner, Maj. F.A. Mitchell, Maj. Lord Apsley, Capt. E.P. Butler, -?-.

Driving and maintenance instruction in camp at Cirencester Park, 1925.

Yeomen at work during Annual Camp at Cirencester Park in July 1925. Hotchkiss gun instruction; this machine-gun, having served the Regiment so well in the First World War, remained a reserve weapon until declared obsolete in 1946, by which time its antiquated design contrasted starkly with the prototypes of the assault-rifle age.

Yeomen at play during Annual Camp at Cirencester Park in July 1925 – blanket tossing.

The officers of 21st (RGH) Armoured Car Coy. in camp at Cirencester Park for annual training, July 1925. Standing, left to right: 2nd Lt. J.S. Sinnott, D. Turner Esq. RAMC, Viscount Elmley, Lt. J. St C. Harvey, 2nd Lt. G.B. Gouldsmith, Capt. H.F.W. Adams RAMC, Lt. W.R. Bailey. Seated: Capt. G.R. Pedder (Adjt.), Capt. R.G. Cullis, Lt.-Col. (QM) S.W. Adderley, Lt.-Col. C.E. Turner DSO TD, Maj. F.A. Mitchell MC (2 i/c), Capt. E.P. Butler, Lt. P.S. Lowsley-Williams.

'Where are we?' The umpires with white hatbands consulting regimental officers on their exact location during an excercise from Cirencester, 1925.

Striking camp at the end of annual training, 1925.

Officer's full dress uniform worn by Captain Sir Anselm Guise in 1927. Lt. Guise had transferred from 3rd Bn. Gloucesters to the RGH in 1912 and went out to join the Regiment in Gallipoli. His family, one of the oldest in Gloucestershire, still reside at Elmore Court.

The officers at Wallingford Camp, August 1928. Standing, left to right: Capt. W.R. Bailey, Lt. J.S. Sinnott, Capt. H.F.W. Adams, 2nd Lt. The Hon. C. Howard, Lt. J. St C. Harvey, 2nd Lt. Lord de Clifford, Lt. Viscount Elmley, Lt. G.J. Yorke, 2nd Lt. R.R.S. Harvey. Seated: Capt. R.G. Cullis, Capt. E.P. Butler, Colonel Duke of Beaufort, Lt.-Col. A.A.N. Beaman DSO, Capt. Lord Apsley DSO MC MP, Capt. H.M. Heyland DSO (Adjt.), Capt. P.S. Lowsley-Williams.

A group of Royal Gloucestershire Hussars at Annual Camp, Tidworth in May 1930. Sitting centre is RSM See (Royal Tanks Corps – Permanent Staff) and on his left CSM Harry Patterson (RGH).

Officers of the 21st (RGH) Armoured Car Coy. at Wheatley Camp, May 1931. Standing, left to right: 2nd Lt. A. Manby-Colgrave, Lt. W.A. Chester-Master, Capt. H.F.W. Adams RAMC, Lt. J. St. C. Harvey, Lt. Lord de Clifford, Capt. J.G. Yorke, Lt. R.R.S. Harvey, Lt. J.S. Sinnott. Seated: Capt. D.J. Mitchell MC, Capt. F.B. Swanwick, Maj. E.P. Butler TD, Maj. F.A. Mitchell MC, Maj. Lord Apsley DSO MC TD, Capt. H.M. Heyland DSO, Capt. P.S. Lowsley-Williams.

Sergeants' Mess of the 21st (RGH) Armoured Car Coy. at Wheatley Camp, May 1931. Standing, left to right: MSSgt. H. Jones, Sgt. J. Hawker, Sgt. F.W. Hodges, Sgt. E.G.T. Farrant, Sgt. R. Geyton, Sgt. O.A. Hill, Sgt. J.A. Clotworthy, Sgt. J.C. Barnes, Sgt. E. Chapple, Sgt. G.A. Lowther. Seated: SSM E. Hearne MM, SSgt. A.R. Hill, CQMS P.W. Hort, CSM R.H. Patterson, Maj. F.A. Mitchell MC, RSM R.A. See, Capt. H.M. Heyland DSO, S/Sgt. J.C. Hort, Sgt. A.G. Hart, SSM R.S. Fisher.

A splendid picture representing the old and the new taken at the gates of Cirencester Park before the Hospital Carnival on 25 July 1931. Captain J.S. Sinnott is in the foreground.

A troop of Rolls Royce armoured cars, *c.* 1931. The cars right and left are crewed by Royal Gloucestershire Hussars, with 11th Hussars in the centre. The officers are, from left to right: Lt. W.A. Chester-Master, Maj. Lord Apsley and Lt. Lord de Clifford. On the extreme left is Maurice Turk, a redoubtable character, and 4th from the right Cpl. Stanley Taylor who was D Sqn SSM at the outbreak of the Second World War.

A group of senior NCOs taken at Annual Camp, Kenilworth in 1933. Standing, left to right: RSM See, RQMS P. Hort, CSM H. Patterson. The seated gentleman has not been identified.

The Tetbury Troop Dispatch Riders at Houghton Down Camp, Stockbridge, August 1934. Captain P.S. Lowsley-Williams is on the left and Sergeant G. Hearsey on the right.

D Sqn off duty outside the canteen, probably at Ashley Arnwood Camp, New Milton, in May 1935. Back row, left to right: -?-, Goodenough, -?-, Hyatt, Tilley, -?-, Miller, Harris, Clark, Eaton, Taylor, Waterman. Seated centre: -?-, McMillan, Woodward, Hort, Watt. Seated front: Hedges, Andrews, Hort, Patterson, Day, Clotworthy, Coleman, Castle, Stevens.

123

A contingent of Royal Gloucestershire Hussars in full dress uniform on parade at Colston Fort, Bristol, *c.* 1935, prior to proceeding to the Colston Hall to take part in the Annual Festival of Remembrance.

Second Lieutenant Bill Hicks Beach on exercise from New Milton Camp, 1935. His family live at Witcombe Park, near Gloucester. He served as a squadron leader in 1st RGH during the Second World War.

The wedding of Jack Clotworthy at Bentworth near Alton, Hampshire, on 9 November 1935. Centre: Jack Clotworthy with Jimmy Watt (Best Man) right and Harry Patterson left. Guard of Honour in full dress uniform with swords, left to right: Stevens, Robbins, Tappenden, Fussell, Newman, Sandell, Coleman, Lewis, Clark, Fenton.

'Stables' on the Rolls Royce armoured cars, probably at Ashley Arnwood Camp, New Milton in May 1935. The Regiment at that time retained one or two armoured cars in each squadron area and was brought up to strength by drawing vehicles from a pool for annual training. The legendary Rolls Royce armoured cars were among the most successful armoured fighting vehicles of all time. They were loved by all who served in them; not only for their romantic associations with Lawrence of Arabia and Glubb Pasha but also for their reliability and versatility. They were originally produced by the Admiralty for the Royal Naval Air Service squadrons in 1914. In 1920 they were modified for service with the Army and the Royal Air Force. Each consisted of a simple body of thin sheet steel built on the Silver Ghost car chassis, later modified in 1924 when the turret cupola was removed. The foreground car is therefore pre-1924. Powered by a six-cylinder Rolls Royce in-line petrol engine developing 40–50 hp they were capable of a road speed of 45 m.p.h. and a range of 180 miles. They were still in use by 11th Hussars in North Africa in 1940–1.

Winners of the Bentinck Cup at Gloucester Barracks, *c.* 1936. Standing, left to right: Weston, -?-, Rea, Taylor, -?-, -?-. Seated, -?-, Sgt. Finch, WO2 Nelson, 2nd Lt. D.J.C. Talbot, L/Cpl. Rumsey, Capt. J.S. Sinnott, RSM See, Sgt. J.C. Barnes, L/Cpl. Dee. Lord Charles Bentinck, 9th Lancers, was Adjutant from 1901–3, during which time he presented a challenge cup to be competed for by yeomanry sections at annual camp.

A Remembrance Day Church Parade at Cirencester in the 1930s. The Royal Gloucestershire Hussars passing the war memorial at the salute with Captain J.S. Sinnott commanding the parade.

RGH Officers in camp at Ashow, Kenilworth in May 1936. On the extreme left, standing, is Capt. R.W.D. Leigh, 11th Hussars (Adjutant) who as Lt.-Col. Lord Leigh commanded 1st RGH from 1943 until the regiment was dispersed by providing reinforcements for the Royal Armoured Corps after the Normandy invasion. Standing, left to right: Capt. R.W.D. Leigh (11th Hussars, Adjutant), Lt. W.A. Chester-Master, 2nd Lt. M.H. Taylor, Lt. Lord de Clifford, 2nd Lt. D.J.C. Talbot, 2nd Lt. Lord St Aldwyn, Lt. R.R.S. Harvey, 2nd Lt. F.R. Perkins, 2nd Lt. W.W. Hicks Beach. Seated: Capt. G.J.C. Yorke, Capt. J. St C. Harvey, Maj. Lord Apsley DSO MC TD MP, Maj. E.P. Butler TD (CO), Capt. P.S. Lowsley-Williams, Maj. H.F.W. Adams RAMC, Capt. J.S. Sinnott.

The D Sqn party leaving Temple Meads station, Bristol to join the regimental contingent of one officer and twenty-one ORs attending the Coronation of King George VI in 1937. Left to right: Tpr. Coleman, L/Cpl. Woodward, SSM Taylor, Cpl. Watt, Sgt. Clotworthy.

A group of officers at Court Farm Camp, Falmer, Sussex in 1938. Left to right: Lt. Lord de Clifford, Maj. Lord Apsley, 2nd Lt. D.J.C. Talbot (back to camera), 2nd Lt. W.W. Hicks Beach, 2nd Lt. Earl St Aldwyn and Lt. M.H. Taylor (back to camera).

RGH Officers in Sussex in May 1938. Seated left is the Adjutant A.T. Smail (11th Hussars) who was seriously disabled while commanding his regiment in Italy. In the summer of 1945 he returned to command and reform 1st RGH for service in the Far East, but eventually the Regiment became part of the Army of Occupation in Austria.

A group of officers photographed at camp in 1938. Lt. Lord de Clifford, 2nd Lt. R.K. Lingard-Guthrie, Lt. M.H. Taylor. Richard Mullings relates a story of the Lingard-Guthries: a regimental if not international incident occurred during 1938 when a party of German students from Gloucester were being given a tour of a typical Cotswold farm. The farm at Tarlton happened to belong to Richard Lingard-Guthrie. The doors of a barn were flung open and there, like a land-borne Q ship, confronting the visitors was the one armoured fighting vehicle then held by the regiment. (A 'Q' ship was a First World War term for an armed ship disguised as a merchantman.)

Windmill Hill – the last camp before the war in July 1939. About one thousand yeomen attended camp after barely three hundred in the previous year.

Pay parade in the rain.

Track training in 'Coffee Pots'.

The private car park.

Motor-cycle power.

Windmill Hill Camp, July 1939. Standing, left to right: Lt. (QM) A.J. Holborow, Lt. W.W. Hicks Beach, Lt. H.R. Rowlands, 2nd Lt. E.H. Milvain, Lt. F.R. Perkins, 2nd Lt. W.E. Barrington-Browne, 2nd Lt. S.L. Lloyd, Capt. J. St C. Harvey, 2nd Lt. J.N. Harper, Lt. M.H. Taylor, Capt. the Revd J.R. Lowe (Chaplain), 2nd Lt. G.C.M. Playne, Lt. D.J.C. Talbot, 2nd Lt. J.H. Cripps, 2nd Lt. A.H. Stanton, 2nd Lt. J.F. Robinson, 2nd Lt. P.H. Cookson, 2nd Lt. J.A.E. Wickes, 2nd Lt. R.K. Lingard-Guthrie, 2nd Lt. D.E.C. Price MFH. Seated: Capt. R. Knight (Adj.), Lt. H.J. Mylne, Capt. The Hon. W.R.S. Bathurst, Capt. Lord de Clifford, Capt. M.K. Braybrook (RAMC), Maj. W.A. Chester-Master, Lt.-Col. J.A.T. Miller OBE, Lt.-Col. E.P. Butler TD, Maj. Lord

Apsley DSO MC TD MP, Capt. P.S. Lowsley-Williams, Maj. J.S. Sinnott, Capt. Lord
Leigh, Capt. G.J. York, Maj. H.F.W. Adams (RAMC), Capt. A.T. Smail (Adjt. 11th
Hussars) MFH. Front: 2nd Lt. R.A.E. Adlard, 2nd Lt. S.A. Pitman, 2nd Lt. T. Willes,
2nd Lt. V.H. Tubbs, Lt. A. Biddulph, 2nd Lt. F.N. Norbury, Lt. D.M. Reinhold, Lt.
Lord Ashton of Hyde MFH, 2nd Lt. A.H. Harford, 2nd Lt. N.D. Hart. It was at this
time that 1st and 2nd lines of the Regiment were formed, which explains why there are
two Commanding Officers, two adjutants and two medical officers in the group. They
were formed on the following areas: 1st RGH – Gloucester, Cirencester and Bristol. 2nd
RGH – Gloucester, Cheltenham, Stroud and Tetbury.

Tent pegging party at Windmill Hill Camp in July 1939. Rear row, left, are three members of a well regarded group from the Vale of Evesham. The two Sale brothers were, in their day, famous swimmers and motor cycle scramblers. Centre rear is Jack Woodger who became a popular and efficient sergeant tank commander. He died of wounds at the Battle of Bir el Gubi in 1941.

A Vickers mark IV light tank photographed at Windmill Hill camp in July 1939. This Mark was the forerunner of the highly successful Mark VIB and VIC models with which the Regiment was fully equipped as a counter-invasion force in 1940–1.

Lunchtime on a middle Sunday of camp. From left to right: Lt. Lord de Clifford, 2nd Lt. Earl St Aldwyn, Miss Diana Turner, and Maj. Tom Butler. Lt.-Col. Jack Miller, in civilian dress, commanded 2nd RGH on the outbreak of war having recently completed his tour commanding 14th/20th Hussars in India. He had married Henry Clifford's widow in 1932.

A Gloucestershire Hussar's wedding. The bridal party leaving St Philip and James' Church, Cheltenham, on Saturday 9 September 1939, after the wedding of Sergeant Lewis Miller, PSI, of the RGH, to Miss Rita Mary Webb, daughter of Mr and Mrs W. Webb of Nailsworth. A number of the bridegroom's comrades were present in uniform.

Rear view of No. 2 College Lawn, Cheltenham, HQ of H Sqn 2nd RGH. The photograph was taken on 3 September 1939 a few moments after the newly mobilized Territorials had listened to Neville Chamberlain announce that Great Britain was at war with Germany. The building is now the Cheltenham Hospital Postgraduate Centre.

D (Bristol) Sqn shortly after mobilization taken at Colston Fort, Bristol, in September 1939. The building was subsequently totally destroyed by enemy air action.
Officers sitting, from left to right: Capt. the Revd J.R. Lowe (Chaplain), Lt. A.H. Harford, Capt. W. Bathurst, Maj. W.A. Chester-Master, Capt. R.R.S. Harvey, Lt. V. Stubbs, Lt. J.R. Robinson. Standing right: Sgt. Jimmy Watt, SSM Stan Taylor and SSM Tug Wilson (Permanent Staff). Most of the ORs present were later commissioned into other, mainly Royal Armoured Corps, regiments.

TRAINING

These men of a mechanised regiment are training hard at a well-known spot. They are very comfortable in their strange quarters, and are obviously determined to add new lustre to a name already distinguished.

1.—The Commanding Officer, Lieut.-Col. E. P. Butler, T.D.

2.—A section of a local troop who are quartered in stables and say they are very comfortable.

3.—Queueing up for dinner rations. The men are extremely well catered for.

4.—Regimental Sergt.-Major J. L. Tytherleigh and Lieut. D. J. C. Talbot.

5.—The guard.

6.—A local squad at marching drill.

7.—Part of a local troop takes a lesson on wireless work and Morse Code.

8.—Checking over details and tools for the Bren gun carriers.

" Cheltenham Chronicle " Photographs. Copies 1/- and 1/9.

A page from the *Cheltenham Chronicle and Gloucestershire Graphic* on Saturday 21 October, 1939 showing 1st RGH training incognito, not far away.

The *Cheltenham Chronicle and Gloucestershire Graphic* being very security minded in October 1939 captioned this photograph 'Somewhere in England'. It shows Lord St Aldwyn, whose father was killed when Adjutant in the unsuccessful relief of A Squadron at Qatia, with the Regimental Chaplain Capt. the Revd J.R. Lowe with dog. They served with 1st RGH.

Ken Lloyd at Market Warsop, Nottinghamshire, in January 1940, with the only tracked vehicle in 2nd RGH, a Vickers Dragon. This was designed and produced by Vickers Carden Lloyd as an artillery tug.

The wireless wing at Cuckney, Nottinghamshire, during the savage winter of January and February 1940. Meals were often taken in the open because the mess-hall on the opposite side of this site was a disused chicken house, too small to provide sufficient seating room for the men of 2nd RGH.

A Vickers Mark II medium tank of 2nd RGH at Edwinstowe in early 1940. This is an early post-First World War tank which entered service in 1926. It was armed with a 3-pounder gun and three .303 in machine-guns and was the first British tank to be fitted with a fully rotating turret. It was used as a training vehicle only and many of them ended their days as anti-invasion pill-boxes in 1940. Pictured from left to right are Frank Griffiths, Tony Holloway, Charles Harnden, Stan Vernon and Ken Wilkins.

2nd RGH found themselves at Skellingthorpe in Lincolnshire during 1940.

A game of cards during a respite from training while in Lincolnshire for men of 2nd RGH.

2nd RGH took over the Cranleigh Motor Company premises in the spring of 1941.
Fitters of the LAD are seen here changing a Dingo's engine.

Springtime in Sussex; H Sqn 2nd RGH at Parham Park, 1941. Standing, left to right:
Roy Perry, Mike Mizon, Ken Lloyd, Ken Caudle. Sitting: John Collins, Bill Welch, John
Ayres.

Getting to know the Crusader. An A15 Cruiser bogged down near Pulborough, Sussex,
February 1941. From here 2nd RGH moved to Warminster for final training before
embarkation.

Sergeant Jim Loveday of 1st RGH, in the driver's hatch, is training crews to drive a Matilda tank. The A12 Mark II Matilda infantry tank was re-designed by Woolwich Arsenal from a 1932 prototype and built in quantity by a number of contractors including Ruston and Hornsby, LMS Railway Works and Harland and Wolff. It filled many differing roles and was the only Allied tank to serve right through the Second World War.

Lakenheath, Suffolk, 1941. Valentine tanks of 1st RGH at an inspection of 6th Armoured Division by HM King George VI. The occasional Matilda can also be seen in the background. The Regiment was due to leave for North Africa with the same division but due to a last minute reorganization both stayed at home and served in a vital training role for the rest of the European war training over five thousand officers and men. Many of its members served with distinction in other regiments all over the world.

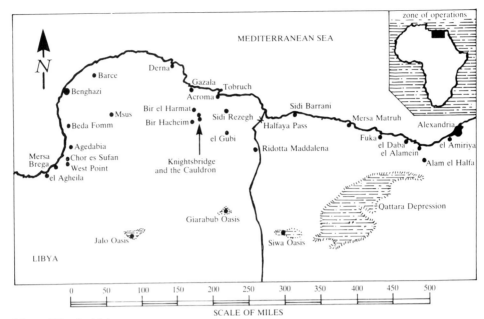

Map of North Africa.

'The Two Types'. Major Jeremy Taylor, H Sqn Leader of 2nd RGH and Trooper Tom Rich MM. The latter was decorated for saving Maj. Rheinhold's tank and crew when the driver was killed during an action in North Africa in 1941.

The main equipment of 2nd RGH in 1940–2 was the Cruiser tank developed from the pre-war Covenanter. It was armed with the standard 2-pounder gun and one 7.92 mm Besa machine-gun, co-axially mounted. In North Africa one tank per squadron was normally fitted with a close support 3 in howitzer to fire smoke or high explosive shot. In 1942 some later models were fitted with the more potent 6-pounder gun, but none of these reached 2nd RGH. The Crusader was powered by the V12 Nuffield Liberty unit, originally a First World War aero engine derated from 400 to 340 hp. It gave the tank an official road speed of 27 m.p.h. but many tank crews, by tinkering with the engine governors, achieved speeds approaching 40 m.p.h. The Crusader was in service with the British army from late 1939 to 1943. In the photograph the circle on the turret identifies the tank as H Sqn, the two (red) pennants as HQ Troop and the square (black) flag as the Sqn Navigator. Pictured from left to right: L/Cpl. K. Smith, Sgt. R. Godwin, Lt. W. Boyd and Maj. W. White.

2nd RGH Crusader approaches a knocked-out Pzkw Mark IV tank. The latter was armed with an 88 mm gun; the Crusader carries the standard British gun of 38 mm calibre. At long range British tanks at this time stood little chance against the heavily armed and armoured opponent.

Early morning on 19 November 1941. 11th Hussars located the Italian Ariete Division with its strong German backing. At Point 181, they marked the spot with a large red flag. 2nd RGH, with H Sqn leading, closed up and the battle was about to begin, No. 4 Troop decided that a photograph should be taken. Leaving the gunners and wireless operators on tank duty, the commanders and drivers posed on open ground before dashing back to their tanks and into action. The Ariete Division, hammered all day by the 22nd Armoured Brigade (2nd RGH, 3 CLY and 4 CLY), were unable to appear again as a fighting force for the remainder of the 1941 operations. This photograph was taken by Cpl. Charlie South the driver, who twenty minutes later was killed in action, becoming the Regiment's first casualty. On the right is Tpr. Jackie Furnivall who was able to restart the tank and under concentrated enemy fire drive it back and prepare it for immediate return to action. For this act he was awarded the Military Medal. The tank commander, Cpl. Bert Vowden, was mentioned in despatches for his part in the exploit. Tim Pitman's history records: 'Lt. Peter Clay, whose tank had broken down at the red flag early in the morning, was asked that evening by the Brigadier to go and find the Commanding Officer. Taking Lt. Bourne's tank and crew he proceeded in the direction of the battle in the failing light, and ran into an anti-tank position and was knocked out and captured. He mystified the Italians for a while as he was dressed entirely in civilian clothes.' He was one of twenty-four captured.

Sunday morning in late December 1941. Shaving, de-sanding and tidying up after the long advance towards Benghazi. The tank is the American M3 Light, generally known as the Honey. It was armed with one 37 mm anti-tank gun and three .3 in Browning machine-guns, one of which was for AA defence. It was powered by a Continental W670 seven-cylinder radial engine and had a road speed of 36 m.p.h. It entered service with the US and British forces in 1941.

Later that same morning and every Sunday, Padre Llewllyn moved around his scattered flock, on this occasion to conduct a pre-Christmas service at el Mechili. Obviously, only a limited number were able to leave their tanks and vehicles at any one time.

How easily the armour was pierced! Note the neat round hole into the side of this tank. Lt. Teddy Milvain, Cpl. Ralph Jones and 2nd Lt. Mike Jeffery after the Battle of Agedabia south of Benghazi in December 1941.

Back in the Nile Delta in March 1942. Battle-experienced 'Desert Rats' refitting and retraining at Beni Yusef before the return to Libya. At the front of the Crusader are, left to right: Monty Rainbow, Eric Johnson (with cigarette), Cpl. Reg Steptoe, 'Rusty' Brookes and Ken Wilkins.

A share-out of rations by a few survivors from knocked out tanks, June 1942.
Somewhere, somehow, Ken Wilkins rescued a small white dog and shared his rations
with it. Not long afterwards Ken was killed in action. Behind him is Sgt. Bill
Brackenbury MM, and, wearing glasses, Sgt. 'Pop' Allies MM.

Knightsbridge. Major Bill Trevor DSO (centre) and the Commanding Officer, Lt.-Col.
'Nat' Birley DSO (right). Both the Colonel and the Adjutant Capt. Muir (left) were
killed in action shortly after the photograph was taken. Maj. Trevor took command of
the Regiment only to be killed by a dive-bomber a short while later. This was a triple
blow from which the Regiment never fully recovered.

The German PzKw Mark IV medium tank. It went into service with the German Army in 1936 and stayed in continuous production throughout the Second World War. It was also used by Italy, Spain and Turkey and by Syria in the 1967 war with Israel. It carried a 75 mm gun, later models carried 88 mm, two 7.92 mm machine guns and had a crew of five. Powered by a Maybach V12 in-line diesel engine developing 300 hp was capable of road speed of 25 m.p.h.. It was the most formidable tank encountered by 2nd RGH. The photograph shows one knocked-out in Libya to the obvious delight of 2nd Lt. Jack Summerell of F Sqn. He was later awarded the MC.

An F Sqn Grant showing its unusual armament arrangement of a 37 mm turret-mounted anti-tank gun and a hull-mounted 75 mm gun for firing high-explosive shot. Big, cumbersome and handicapped by the limited traverse of its main armament it nevertheless was the first allied tank to offer some degree of parity with the Mark III's and Mark IV's of the Afrika Korps.

Brothers in arms. Occasionally one finds two brothers in one squadron, rarely in the same troop – two in the same tank crew must be almost unique. Here Bob Bayliss, standing far left, and brother Charlie Bayliss, standing third from left, pose in front of their F Sqn Grant. Their tank is mounted on a transporter ready for the long haul from Egypt to their position in the Gazala line to await the coming battles at Knightsbridge and the Cauldron.

Halcyon days. There were moments of great peace when the desert was silent, the air clear and not a fly within ten miles. A Crusader crew take their midday meal, probably the usual but ever popular bully-beef stew, or could it have been the greatest delight of all – tinned pineapple chunks?

German Mk III. Here, the crew of a G Sqn Crusader examine a German Pzkw Mark III tank. This particular version carries a long barrelled 75 mm gun. The large container on the back of the British tank is an auxiliary petrol tank. The fuel in it would normally be used for approach marches. It could be jettisoned from within when in action.

A Messerschmidt fighter shot down in the regimental area near Alamein in August 1942. Tpr. Moulden (in cockpit), Tpr. Wathen and Cpl. Clutterbuck.

Billowing sand about to engulf 2nd RGH tented camp site at Sidi Bishr, near Alexandria.

The Three Musketeers. Junior NCOs, Cpls Frank Griffiths (who had escaped from captivity a few days earlier), Doug Price and Tony Holloway. The trio, with Oscar Green, escaped from encircling enemy forces in the abandoned truck they had recovered from a minefield. At some point they 'found' the Australian hats which gave protection from the mid-summer sun. They all agreed that the most hair-raising part of the day had been Oscar's driving. Twenty years later Tony Holloway became the Commanding Officer of the Regiment.

Winston Churchill inspected the Alamein Line in August 1942 and before leaving paused to present gallantry medals to men of 2nd RGH. Shortly after the Axis forces attacked, precipitating the Battle of Alam Halfa, later to be known as First Alamein. During this critical action a force of 2nd RGH yeomen formed a fighting squadron of 5th Royal Tank Regiment. Pictured in the staff car are Lt.-Gen. Sir Brian Horrocks and the Prime Minister. Standing, left to right, are SSM Gardner, Maj. M.H. Taylor, Sgt. W. Brackenbury MM, Sgt. H. Webber and Cpl. W.A.A.G. Poole MM.

The Prime Minister was also introduced to other decorated men of the regiment. He is seen shaking hands with Major N. King MC.

The spirit of the 8th Army. After the disaster of Knightsbridge, the long retreat of 1942 ended at the approaches to Alexandria. On 31 August the Axis forces made their last attempt to destroy the 8th Army, occupy the Nile Delta and seize the Suez Canal. All three fighting squadrons of 2nd RGH took a hand in the dogged battle centred on Alam Halfa until 3 September when the enemy, exhausted and short of supplies, called it a day. This battle, brilliantly conducted by General Auckinleck, marked the turning point of the war in North Africa; it was also 2nd RGH's last action as a regiment. However, the majority of its yeomen, with other regiments and far better equipment, fought on through Italy, France, Belgium, Holland and Germany. Our picture shows Sgt. Charles A. 'Bear' of H Sqn. A former policeman, he was also a great rugby player, and an efficient and ever-popular tank commander. He was awarded the Military Medal for rescuing his troop leader 2nd Lt. J.R. Proctor at the Battle of Knightsbridge and was later commissioned into the Royal Tank Regiment. His portrait can be seen on the inn sign over the Yeoman Hotel in Southgate Street, Gloucester. The original sketch drawn by Eric Johnson is shown above.

...in all, "Trouble"

Always a very keen motor cycle trials rider, Major Jeremy Taylor laid out a circuitous course around the regimental camp at Sidi Bishr in 1942. This WD BSA is being attended to by John Willie and Jeremy Taylor (centre), Tim Slee and 'Simon' look on.

An ingenious weapon was devised in the desert by the officers and SNCOs which was christened the Taylor-Higgs AA Gun.

This H Sqn group was taken just before the Regiment was disbanded in September 1942 at Sidi Bishr near Alexandria.

The Alamein cemetery for British, Commonwealth and Allied troops killed defending the Nile Delta, Alexandria and the Suez Canal. The photograph, taken in 1943, shows part of the burial ground under construction. At that time ten thousand graves had already been marked out.

1st RGH being inspected by the Honorary Colonel the Duke of Beaufort, at Bury St Edmunds in September 1945 prior to their departure for Austria. Officers from left to right are: Col. the Duke of Beaufort, Maj. John Talbot, Lt.-Col. Trevor Smail, Lt.-Col. Charles Turner (in civilian dress).

Capt. Bill Barrington Browne (left) served with 2nd RGH during the Second World War. He was posted to the Armoured Corps Rangers as a staff officer. He became a well-known sporting artist in later years, living at Coberley near Cheltenham. His wife Cecilia, was the eldest daughter of Cecil Elwes and their son Dominic, having served in the Royal Dragoons, became Adjutant of the Wessex Yeomanry on formation in 1971 and has been Regimental Secretary from then to the present day. He is thus a fourth generation Gloucestershire Hussar and was clearly going to follow in father's footsteps from an early age.

A Sqn Officers 1st RGH at Ogbourne St George Camp in 1942. From left to right, standing: Lt. H. Blowfield, Lt. A. Biddulph, Lt. H. Braithwaite; seated, -?-, Capt. P. Loram, Maj. W.W. Hicks Beach, Capt. D.J.C. Talbot, Lt. F.R. Perkins.

Capt. Norman Hart was an instructor at the Royal Military Academy at Sandhurst after service in North Africa with 2nd RGH. He is pictured here seated third from the left. His son Christopher served as a squadron leader in the 1970s and his grandson Simon served as a troop leader in the 1980s.

A Sqn 1st RGH in Austria 1946. In the foreground is a US Greyhound armoured car and in the background Sherman tanks. The Sherman, a US M4 medium tank, was the first tank in the British Army to carry a respectable gun, 75 mm. It was powered by a Ford GAA V8 engine which gave it a road speed of 26 m.p.h. and carried a crew of five. The Sherman entered service in 1942 and was used by most allied armies during the Second World War, but sadly too late for 2nd RGH in North Africa.

Recce Troop of 1st RGH in Austria in 1946. The vehicles shown here are US Greyhound armoured cars. The Regiment had been trained and prepared to go to the Far East, but after the atomic bomb was dropped in Japan they were sent to Austria as part of the army of occupation.

1st RGH in Austria. These yeomen are on border guard during their spell with the army of occupation in 1946.

The mounted troop of 1st RGH about to perform the Musical Ride at the British Army Tattoo in Austria in 1946 in front of the Schönbrunn Palace, Vienna. All the horses were requisitioned locally and the full dress uniforms were sent out from England for the occasion. Captain Risby the Quartermaster is the officer in charge.

Two Daimler armoured cars of the RGH in front of Regimental Headquarters at
Gloucester Barracks, *c.* 1950. The cars, light reconnaissance vehicles, carried the same
armament as the Crusader tanks used by the regiment in 1941–2. The Daimler had a road
speed of 50 m.p.h. and, due to an unconventional gearbox, was capable of a similar
speed in reverse. The Daimler was in service in the British Army from 1941 to 1960. The
barracks have been demolished for redevelopment.

The RGH darts team. Winners of the Old Comrades Darts Association Final versus the
Guards Association at the Empire Hall, North Street, Cheltenham in 1950. Standing, left
to right: Roy Weeks, Eric Greenwood, George Richards, Les Tarren. Front row: Alf
Wiggall, Roy Perry, Arthur Harris MM, Ron Deane, John Fluck.

A Daimler armoured car buried under a group of officers and men at annual camp at Lulworth in 1956. Among the officers are Lt. J.F. Heaton and Lt. W.A.M. Mitchell on top, with Lt. M.J.T. Martineau, Capt. the Earl Bathurst and Capt. P. Shimwell standing. On the extreme left is the redoubtable SSM McKenna.

Lieutenant Colonel G.P. Shakerley MC TD of Moreton-in-Marsh and later Sevenhampton, commanded the Regiment 1951/3, having won his MC with the Rifle Brigade Territorials during the war. He was chairman of the County Council from 1955–67, High Sheriff in 1961 and was knighted in 1972.

RGH Officers at annual camp at Kirkcudbright in May 1952. They wear black armbands in mourning for King George VI. From left to right, back row: 2nd Lt. M.E. Jones, 2nd Lt. C.V.B. Eardley-Wilmot, 2nd Lt. M. Evans, 2nd Lt. M. Morris, 2nd Lt. J. Barnard, 2nd Lt. Bing, 2nd Lt. J.B. Bryant, 2nd Lt. J.D. Bryant, Lt. the Earl Bathurst, Lt. T. Stock. Middle row: 2nd Lt. Chamberlain, Lt. the Hon. T.J. Ashton, Capt. R.G. Hyde MC, Capt. R. Thompson, Capt. J. de C. Mitchell, Capt. M.F. Carter, Lt. C. Ward, Capt. A.A.L. Holloway. Front row: Maj. W.E. Jerden MBE (Quartermaster), Capt. R.D. Sutton, (11th Hussars, Adjutant), Maj. P.F.S. Clifford, Maj. S.R.M. Jenkins (4th/7th Dragoon Guards), Lt.-Col. G.P. Shakerley MC TD, Maj. G.R. Coleman MC TD, Maj. A. Biddulph TD, Capt. R. Freeman Thomas, Capt. E. Milvain MC, Capt. the Revd H. Heal.

D Sqn contingent at the Coronation of HM Queen Elizabeth II, June 1953. From left to right, standing: Cpl. Hall, Tpr. Heydon. Seated: Tpr. Hatch, Sgt. Parsons, Cpl. Barlow.

Her Majesty The Queen at Shire Hall during her official visit to Gloucester in 1953. Between the yeomen of the RGH forming the Guard of Honour are from left to right: HM The Queen, His Grace the Duke of Beaufort (Lord Lieutenant), Colonel Godman (Chairman of the County Council) and HRH the Duke of Edinburgh. Colonel John Godman had been posted to the RGH as Adjutant (1914–16) from 15th Hussars. (His operation order can be seen on p. 54 for the landing at Suvla Bay, Gallipoli in 1915.) He commanded 15th/19th Hussars 1926–30 and became High Sheriff in 1942. He was chairman of the County Council from 1946–56, and lived at Loughborough.

Kirkcudbright, 1955. At this time the Regiment was fully equipped with Daimler armoured cars. Here is one stuck firmly in the ditch. If recovery within the troop's own resources did not work, the squadron LAD heavy recovery would have been called upon.

Rollestone Camp, Salisbury Plain, 1957. The Duke of Beaufort inspecting the guard on the middle Sunday of camp followed by Lieutenant Colonel. J.A. Kershaw MC MP, the Commanding Officer. Anthony Kershaw had won his MC with 16th/5th Lancers in Tunisia during the war. He was Member of Parliament for Stroud from 1955 until 1987.

Below:
HM The Queen at Badminton Three Day Event, 1959. Accompanying Her Majesty is Col. Cox Cox and behind him can be seen HM The Queen Mother and HRH the Princess Margaret. Sgt. May RGH is on the right.

Castlemartin, 1959. Maj. 'Slip' Mitchell's HQ Squadron on the ranges in South Wales.
Trailer No. 4: Sgt. Kennedy, TQMS Truss, Sgt. Barrett, L/Cpl. Pinnell, RQMS Webster,
Sgt. Matthews. Trailer No. 3: L/Cpl. Cook, SSM Scott, Tpr. Townsend, Tpr. Harris,
Tpr. Holden, Tpr. Phillips. Trailer No. 2: Capt. the Hon. T.J. Ashton, Capt. D.B.
Money-Coutts, Lt. J.F. Heaton, Maj. J. de C. Mitchell. Trailer No. 1: Tpr. Johns,
SQMS Smith, Sgt. Sinton, Tpr. Niven, Cpl. Chivers, Tpr. Timbrell, S.Sgt. Long. Austin
Champ: Tpr. Powell, L/Cpl. Halliday, Tpr. Pearce, Tpr. Bailey, Sgt. Pearce, Tpr.
Halliday, Cpl. Ponting, L/Cpl. Cotterell.

Lt. David Lowsley-Williams raised 4 Troop B Sqn in Tetbury in 1960. Training nights
were held in the skittle alley of the 'Royal Oak' by invitation of Mr Walter Baker,
(ex-RGH) whose two sons were active members of the Squadron. Laughed at by some as
the 'Tetbury Teds', 4 Troop won the Mitchell Cup for the Inter-Troop Competition at
annual camp at Lulworth in 1961. Back row: Tprs C. Lyddieth, J. Ball, L/Cpl. S. West,
Tprs L. Gwinnett, G. Maddy, D. Cooper. Front row: L/Cpl. J. Wood, Sgt. E. Tucker,
Lt. D. Lowsley-Williams, Maj. M. St Clair, Cpl. A.R. Perrins, L/Cpl. G. Fenney. The
officers are wearing Beaufort Blue dress caps with a buff band. Dress caps changed to
crimson for the Guidon Parade, 1962.

A survivor of the Battle of Qatia. Captain Charles Lovell MBE receiving a silver model of a mounted hussar from Colonel the Duke of Beaufort at Lulworth Camp in 1961. Charles Lovell, a long serving yeoman of the RGH, was gravely wounded at Qatia and left for dead. He was later found among a heap of corpses by an Australian Medical Officer who flew him back to the nearest casualty clearing station where his right leg was amputated at the knee. On returning to England he busied himself corresponding with everyone he knew in the Regiment, keeping in touch with each one until they had all returned home. With this nucleus of names he set up the Comrades Association which thrived under his enthusiasm for the next fifty years.

Too many cooks! Grub up for men of Lt. Piers Birchall's troop of B Sqn at Lulworth in 1961. Cpl. D. Vaile is official taster on his troop leader's right and Tpr. M. Marsden is squatting at the back. Sgt. N. F. Hall is on the extreme left.

Qatia Day in 1966 on College Green, Gloucester. Front, from left to right: Lt. J.D. Birchall, Maj. W.A. Mitchell, SSM E.L. Pearce, Capt. P.E.D. Birchall. Ted Pearce's two sons are both currently serving.

169

The Guidon Presentation Ceremony, May 1962. The Hon. Colonel inspecting the Regiment in front of Badminton House. From left to right: Maj. R.C.T. Sivewright MC, Lt.-Col. A.A.L. Holloway TD DL, Col. Sir Geoffrey Shakerley CBE MC TD DL and Col. the Duke of Beaufort.

The Guidon Presentation Ceremony. Col. the Duke of Beaufort, representing HM The Queen, presents the Guidon to Sgt. B.N. Rose. The escorts are: rear, SSM Birtwhistle; foreground, SSM Smith. The officer with his back to the camera is Col. Sir Geoffrey Shakerley, the Deputy Honorary Colonel.

RSM Hall at Badminton, 1962. Nobby Hall's remarkable military career was divided between 11th Hussars and RGH: enlisted as band boy 11th Hussars 1932, Troop Sgt. 11th Hussars 1939, Troop SM to Dick Sutton 11th Hussars in Normandy 1945, PSI D Sqn RGH, RSM RGH, RSM 11th Hussars, QM 11th Hussars, QM RGH, QM Royal Hussars, QM Wessex Yeomanry as a major. One of his sons joined 11th Hussars and another joined the RGH.

In 1963 the Regiment was presented with the Freedom of Entry to the City of Gloucester. Here the Mayor takes the salute as the parade moves up Eastgate Street towards the Cross. Behind the five mounted yeomen come three Ferret scout cars, followed by the regimental band, the Regiment marching by squadrons and finally the Old Comrades.

C Sqn on exercise, 1963. From left to right: L/Cpl. D. Cook, L/Cpl. R. Langford, Lt. J.D. Rees, Capt. P.N. Ayshford-Sanford, Capt. the Hon. T.M. Ponsonby.

C Sqn SHQ. Sergeant B. Coburn and the Austin 1-ton 'rear link' vehicle.

B Sqn at Folkestone Camp, 1963. SSM E.L. Pearce, SQMS D. Baker, Sgt. A.L. Perrins and Austin command vehicles.

Trooper H. Hughes with his B Sqn water-truck.

SQMS Ron Doane with C Sqn's truck.

HQ Sqn team, winners at the Regimental Rifle Meeting, Sneedhams Green, 1963. From left to right: Sgt. K.F. Millington, Cpl. R. Wyman, Cpl. Bailey, SSM R. Smith (with Pitman Cup), Sgt. Matthews, Sgt. R.F. Pearce (with Gallop and Shenton Trophy for best individual shot), ? Bailey, RQMS J. Smith, Cpl. J. Timbrell (with shield for Bren Pairs), Tpr. R.C. Smith, Tpr. Bradley, Sgt. Cheeseman (RAPC).

A troop of B Sqn (Stroud and Tetbury), Penhale Camp, 1964. From left to right, Tpr. D. Minter, Sgt. E. Tucker, Lt. J. Comins (Ex 8th Hussars), Cpl. C. Lyddieth, Tpr. G. Maddy, L/Cpl. S. West. In 1955 Daimler armoured cars were withdrawn. Daimler scout cars (Dingos) stayed for a few years. By 1960 all the Dingos had gone, and each squadron had a troop of three Ferret scout cars, the other troops mounted in Austin Champs and, later, Landrovers. The No. 19 wireless set was still in use. Battle dress or denim overalls were worn on training. RGH was the Divisional Recce Regiment of 43 (Wessex) Infantry Division.

Another troop of B Sqn, 1964. Sgt. R.E. Davies in the turret of a Ferret. This picture includes: L/Cpl. D. Begley, Tpr. Robbins, Tpr. Cook, L/Cpl. Clapham, Cpl. D. Powis.

The Duke of Beaufort trying out the new SLR (self-loading rifle) at Cranwich Camp, Norfolk, 1965. The instructor was SSM B. Hart of C Sqn.

At annual camp, Thetford, 1965, RQMS M. Williams on behalf of the serving regiment presented the Duke of Beaufort with a new saddle, to mark his forty years as Honorary Colonel, and Mr Charles Lovell presented the Duke with a new bridle, from the Comrades Association. From left to right: Lt.-Col. R.C.T. Sivewright MC (Commanding Officer), Mr Charles Lovell, RQMS Williams, Duke of Beaufort, RSM Sharpe (11H). In the background: Sgt. Cheeseman, Sgt. May, Sgt. McKenna.

The Severn Bridge, 8 September 1966. Full Dress Orderlies in front of the Royal Stand for the opening of the new bridge by Her Majesty The Queen. From left to right: Sgts Pearce, Hare, Coburn, L/Cpl. Mackie, Begley, Roffe, Tprs A. Curtis, G. Curtis.

In April 1967, the TA in Gloucestershire was reorganized again, with RGH providing the nucleus of a Home Defence Unit for Gloucestershire and Bristol. Volunteers joined from 5th Glosters, North Somerset & Bristol Yeomanry, and the Gloucestershire Volunteer Artillery to form squadrons based in Cheltenham, Cirencester and Bristol. Equipment and training scales were much reduced, eight days camp per year and two weekends. In the photograph the Duke of Beaufort inspects the regiment, with Lt.-Col. M.A.J. St Clair accompanied by Maj. C.F.L. Boyce (ex 5th Glosters), Capt. D.R. Ayshford Sanford, Maj. The Hon. T.M. Ponsonby. Tpr. M. Marsden is left marker of the rank being inspected.

In 1969 the Territorial Army was reorganized once again and RGH was reduced to a cadre of three officers and five SNCOs. Their job was to look after regimental property and to keep themselves 'alive' to provide a base for expansion at some future date. Also in 1969, four officers and some fifty yeomen volunteered to form a troop of 37 (Wessex & Welsh) Signal Regiment, based on the former RGH Drill Hall in Cheltenham. In early 1971, members of the cadre were told to plan to raise RHQ, A, C and HQ Sqns of a new regiment, to be called the Wessex Yeomanry. B and D Sqns were to be raised by the cadres of the Royal Wiltshire Yeomanry and the Royal Devon Yeomanry. From left to right: Capt. C.N. Hart, Capt. D. Lowsley-Williams, S.Sgt. B.N. Rose, Maj. the Hon T.M. Ponsonby, Sgt. J. White, WO2 R. Pearce, Sgt. E. Tucker, Sgt. R. Bastin at a gathering at the newly named Royal Gloucestershire Hussars pub at Frocester.

The Cadre on a liaison visit to 11th Hussars at Tidworth during their annual camp in 1969. On the Centurion tank from left to right: S.Sgt. B.N. Rose, Sgt. R. Bastin, Sgt. R.E. Winter. Standing: WO2 R. Pearce, Capt. C.N. Hart, Maj. The Hon T.M. Ponsonby, Capt. D. Lowsley-Williams.

Corporal C.J. Etheridge prepares for a mounted recce with men of A Sqn. He rose to the rank of RQMS as a yeoman and then transferred to the Permanent Staff and is still serving.

Annual Camp, 1974. Jurby on the Isle of Man was the furthest from home to date. Sgt. M.M.W. Marsden, Tprs Bennett, Horton and L/Cpl. Curtis on patrol, no weapons allowed. Sgt. Marsden joined G Sqn, as it then was, in Stroud in 1959. He rejoined in 1971, was promoted to SSM then RQMS, later commissioned as MTO and is now HQ Sqn. Leader. At one time he had two brothers and a son in C Sqn.

Wessex Yeomanry Warrant Officers' and Sergeants' Mess, Annual Camp at Crowborough, Sussex in 1975. From left to right, back row: Sgt. Crook, Sgt. Jack Wickes, S/Sgt. Perkins (3RTR), Sgt. John Wickes, Sgt. Burnett. Third row: Sgt. Vaughan, Sgt. Plastow, Sgt. Dudman, Sgt. Rose, Sgt. Jackson, Sgt. Armstrong, Sgt. Lewis, Sgt. Perry. Second row: S/Sgt. Lambert, Sgt. Bird, Sgt. Robinson, Sgt. Cunningham, Sgt. Stocks, Sgt. Horsell, Sgt. Marsden, Sgt. Hird, Sgt. Shepherd, S/Sgt. Simms, S/Sgt. Walker, WO2 Rose. Front row: S/Sgt. Coles, S/Sgt. Garlick (RH), WO2 Black (ACC), WO2 Smith, RQMS Tucker, RSM Birch, Lt.-Col. Lowsley-Williams, WO2 Mitchell, WO2 Dawson, WO2 Hawkins, S/Sgt. Wherton (RH), S/Sgt. Humberstone (RH). Bernard Humberstone was later RSM Royal Hussars, and then returned to Gloucestershire to the Royal Wessex Yeomanry.

Wessex Yeomanry Officers, Annual Camp at Cultybraggan, Perthshire in 1976. At Rear:
O/Cdt. N. Agg-Manning, O/Cdt. M. Boxall, The Hon. R.I. Wills, 2nd Lt. R.C.
Ponsonby, O/Cdt. C. Lees, Mr T. Arden, Capt. G.D. Stephenson (RAPC), Lt. C.P.
Ross, Lt. J.F. Penley, Capt. M.J. Avis, Lt. S.D.E. Parsons, Capt. the Visct. Ullswater,
Maj. L.M. Humphreys (RAMC), Capt. R.L. Jenkins, Lt. W.A.A. Wells, Lt. the Lord
Courtenay, 2nd Lt. J.S. Selby-Bennett. Seated: Maj. J.A. Hall (QM), Maj. J.M.N.
Powell (QRIH), Capt. P.R.H. Clifford, Maj. S. Biddulph, Maj. D. Shaw (RH), Lt.-Col.
P.E.D. Birchall, Maj. C.N. Hart, Maj. N.F.A. Page-Turner, Maj. J.A.P. Forbes, Maj.
D.S. Barrington-Browne.

Annual Camp in 1977 was at Sennybridge in Wales. There were excellent infantry
training facilities, but it was very cold and wet. Sergeant B. Marsden (C Sqn) explains
the next section of the individual battle run to Trooper Gray.

Mrs David Lowsley-Williams presenting Lt. Rupert Ponsonby with the cup for the first serving officer, after the Yeomanry Ride at Frampton-on-Severn, 26 November 1978. The overall winner was Capt. Mark Phillips (late QDG). Maj. Victor Seely, Royal Hussars, Training Major, looks on. He had served as Adjutant to the RGH in 1965/6 as an 11th Hussar.

In 1978 and in 1981 the Wessex Yeomanry sent a composite squadron, chosen from the four squadrons of the Regiment, to Gibraltar for two weeks, to relieve one company of the regular infantry battalion who were on permanent garrison duty. Members of C Sqn from Cirencester and Stroud are seen at the Air Mounting Centre, South Cerney before flying to Gibraltar in March 1978. Included in the picture are the following NCOs and yeomen: Cross, Morley, Kilby, Walker, Ricalton, Luce, Wood, Stratford, Brunsdon, Fordyce, Apperley, Hicks, Day and Debenham.

Sgt Bird of A Sqn checking respirators of the Gloucester men during gas training as part of their preparation for the two-week exercise in Gibraltar.

Governors Guard

As well as using the excellent training facilities tunnelled into the Rock, the composite squadron took its turn guarding the border with Spain and providing a Ceremonial Guard at The Convent, the residence of the Governor and Commander in Chief. Convent Guard: Sgt. G.W. Ponting, L/Cpl. R. Kirby, Tpr. D. Kilby, L/Cpl. R. Ford, Cpl. W. Brunsdon.

Sherston Cross Country Team Event, 23 March 1977. The Regiment entered a team of four riders for this equestrian event in the Beaufort Country: Maj. Simon Biddulph (C Sqn. Leader) is seen above jumping the big wall. Maj. Johnny Powell (QRIH), the Training Major; Capt. Charles Mann (C Sqn, 2 i/c) and Maj. Rollo Clifford (A Sqn Leader), were placed 7th out of a large entry.

Army Downhill Skiing Championships, Ischgl, Austria, January 1980. Since the mid-1970s the Wessex Yeomanry have sent a team to compete against the Regular Army teams in Austria. The HAC was the only other territorial regiment to compete. The team in 1980 was: Maj. Rollo Clifford (A Sqn), Capt. Chris Lees (B Sqn RWY), Capt. Andy Hodson (A Sqn), Lt. Willie Colville (A Sqn) and Capt. Andrew Maitland (C Sqn).

The Duke of Beaufort, Honorary Colonel, inspecting C Sqn at Knook Camp, Warminster in May 1980, escorted by Major J.V. Eyre, commanding C Sqn and Lt.-Col. D.R. Ayshford-Sanford.

Lt. Simon Hart, master and huntsman of the Royal Agricultural College Beagles, talking to the Duke of Beaufort at a meet near Badminton, 10 January 1984. This was the last public appearance of the 10th Duke before his death a short while later. Simon Hart was a third generation yeoman.

A (RGH) Sqn The Royal Wessex Yeomanry, Penhale Camp, 1983.

C (RGH) Sqn The Royal Wessex Yeomanry, Penhale Camp, 1983

In 1981 and 1987 the Royal Wessex Yeomanry sent a composite squadron made up of troops from each of the four squadrons, to the USA to train with the National Guard. Lt. Henry Ashton with the C Sqn troop in Pennsylvania with SSM Mick Marsden at his feet. He has S/Sgt. Brian Marsden on his left and Sgt. Andy Beard on his right.

Lieutenant Andy Hodson of A Sqn at Fort Indian Town Gap, Pennsylvania, USA, 1981. The Squadron was hosted by the Maryland National Guard who sent one company to England to work with RWxY at their annual camp at Knook.

Taunton Polo Club, May 1987. The Royal Wessex Yeomanry regimental team had just beaten the Royal Navy in a friendly encounter before the Inter-Regimental Polo Tournament. Capt. Guy Hankin ('B' Sqn RWY), Lt.-Col. Rollo Clifford, Maj. Christopher Le Hardy (13/18H Training Major and umpire), Lt. Tim Verdon (B Sqn RWY; formerly RGH), Capt. Andrew Kerr (A Sqn).

'Roncamp' at Pauntley Court, home of Lt.-Col. David Ayshford-Sanford. These annual weekend camps are based on the comforts supplied by ex-SQMS Ron Doane and are attended by a band of senior yeomen each year. Left to right: Doug Gerrard, Tony Holloway, Ken Smith, Ken Lloyd, Keith Mann and Doug Price. The standard to be raised is the same one that flew over 2nd RGH camp at Sidi Bishr in Egypt in 1942.

The Fisher Ground at Tidworth, August 1990. After thirteen years of competing the Royal Wessex Yeomanry finally won one of the two military polo tournaments. The Captains and Subalterns team beat the Blues and Royals in the final, 5½ – 5 goals. This was the first time a yeomanry team had won the Queen's Bays Cup since its inception in 1897. Pictured from left to right: Capt. Alex Dabell (B Sqn. RWY), Lt. Jamie Gordon (C Sqn.), Gen. Sir John Chapple GCB CBE ADC, John Warren of the sponsors Laurent-Perrier, Lt. Tim Verdon (B Sqn. RWY) and Capt. Paul Lucas (QOH and Adjutant).

The official opening of the Regiments of Gloucestershire Museum by HRH the Duke of Gloucester, Colonel in Chief the Gloucestershire Regiment, accompanied by The Duke of Beaufort, Honorary Colonel Royal Gloucestershire Hussars, 24 June 1990. HRH is moving to the right, escorted by General Sir John Waters, Colonel of the Gloucesters. Lt.-Col. J.F. Penley greets HRH the Duchess of Gloucester with the Lord Lieutenant Colonel Tim Gibbs. Col. J.E.B. Hills, County High Sheriff, is in the background.

C Sqn's Cambrian Patrol team, 1989. From left to right, standing: Tpr. Rice, Cpl. Moore, Cpl. Wheeler, Lt. A.J.O. Martin. Kneeling centre: L/Cpl. Hancock, Tpr. Hordern. Kneeling front: O/Cdt. Scarlett, Tpr. Temlett, O/Cdt. Attwell. Alistair Martin was patrol leader and lives at the Target, previously the Target Inn, near Stroud.

ACKNOWLEDGEMENTS

During the setting up of the Regiments of Gloucestershire Museum in the docks at Gloucester in 1990, Mr David Smurthwaite, Assistant Director of the National Army Museum, remarked that the RGH had as fine a collection of historical photographs of any regiment, regular or territorial, that he had seen. This inspired a reaction from the Regimental Trustees, which led to the Museum Layout Committee 'volunteering' to compile this book in order to save the photographs from oblivion. As chairman of this small committee, I found myself an 'author', despite the team effort that put it together.

Piers Birchall, Paul Clarke, Dick Coleman, Tony Holloway and Eric Johnson were the experts of their time who produced the material and the vital information from which the captions were written. Tony Mitchell assisted by writing the Introduction while Dominic Barrington-Browne provided direction throughout.

Special thanks must go to the families of the great attics of Gloucestershire for allowing us to raid their treasures; the Duke of Beaufort at Badminton, Lord Apsley from Cirencester Park, Lord Neidpath of Stanway, my mother from Frampton, Charles Lloyd-Baker at Hardwicke.

Documents of particular help were lent by Mrs Elizabeth Suckling (Sir Algar Howard's diary) and Col. Sir Piers Bengough (his uncle's papers) and photograph albums from the Hon. Tom Ponsonby (Lord de Mauley's), The Hon. George Bathurst for his father's photographs, the Rt. Revd Bill Llewellyn, Major Jeremy Taylor and Mr Paul Clarke. The Royal Wessex Yeomanry scrap books were also most useful.

I have quoted extensively from Frank Fox's regimental history, and used as a source the works of W.H. Windham-Quin, Sir Lionel Darell, Lt.-Col. Tim Pitman and Richard Mullings.

My thanks for their memories to Col. Tim Gibbs, Henry Elwes, Wing-Commander Fred Winterbotham, Mrs Keith Dunn, Sir Robin Dunn and Brigadier Roscoe Harvey.

Many excellent loose photographs were lent by Tom Hall, Miss Colburn, Simon Hart, Jim Loveday, Tony Broxton, Ted Lord, Ian Shaw, Doug Gerrard, Andy Hodson, Ken Lloyd and Ken Smith. The following also agreed to let us use their photographs: Brian Berkeley, Peter Harding, John Kimpton, Jack Clotworthy, Arthur Harris. Other material was provided by both the Dean and the Mayor of Gloucester, John Penley, Andrew Kerr, Patrick Polglase, Stan Bywater and Anthony Hart. Both *The Citizen*, The Cheltenham and Bailey Group Newspapers, allowed me to tap their resources as did the County Archivist Mr David Smith without whose help the Walwin album, upon which we have drawn so heavily, would never have come to light.

Last but not least, our thanks go to our patient typist, Caroline Ractliffe and our loyal band of proof-readers.